SECRET
PHILADELPHIA

A GUIDE TO THE WEIRD, WONDERFUL, AND OBSCURE

Mary Dixon Lebeau

Library of Congress Control Number: 2017958840

ISBN: 9781681061344

Design by Jill Halpin

Printed in the United States of America
18 19 20 21 22   5 4 3 2 1

DEDICATION

My mother taught me to love this city, and my father taught me to love the writing process; my children—Courtney, Steven, Sean, Max and Libby—taught me to always see things with new eyes.

This book is dedicated to them, and especially to Scott, my partner on this journey and the keeper of my secrets.

"For in the darkness, will be hidden worlds that shine."
—Bruce Springsteen

CONTENTS

INTRODUCTION

When I first approached writing *Secret Philadelphia*, I thought it would be a challenge. After all, this is America's birthplace, the City of Brotherly Love and Sisterly Affection. It's a favorite class trip destination and the stuff of middle-school history books. So much about this city—the good and the not-so-much—is well known. We're the Liberty Bell, Rocky Balboa, soft pretzels, and the fans who throw snowballs at Santa. Is there anything about Philly that's secret?

Flash forward a few months, and I found myself hiking through the wilderness near Wissahickon Creek, searching for the cave of a doomsday cult. Surrounded by the lush green, I felt so remote, so isolated, so unlike the vibe one usually feels in a major city. I whispered to my husband, "It's hard to believe we're in Philadelphia." But we were.

I found myself saying the same thing, over and over again, as I explored this city I thought I knew. I sought out the stories never mentioned on the typical school trips and learned that we're so much more than the Liberty Bell and Betsy Ross. Each neighborhood presented its own treasures—from dueling restaurants to singing fountains and from Japanese cherry blossoms to Tastykake apple pie. Art is around every corner (literally), and inspiration can be found in the churchyards and cemeteries. I took a train tour through nostalgia and was dwarfed by clothespins and paintbrushes. I saw a collection of glittery New Year's costumes and fell in love with the beauty of broken glass. And I stood where Ben Franklin stood (almost unavoidable—he's everywhere!).

Yes, this is Philadelphia—this and so much more. Listen as I share some secrets with you . . . then head out to uncover a few of your own.

¹WHERE THE DINOSAURS ROAM

Where can you find America's oldest natural science museum?

Founded in 1812, the Academy of Natural Sciences of Drexel University is the country's oldest natural history research institution and museum. Many local kids remember the museum as the place where they wandered through room after room of dioramas featuring wildlife in their natural habitats. The dioramas display an assortment of animals, from panda to wildebeest and from gorilla to moose.

But even the massive moose seems small when compared to the creatures roaming Dinosaur Hall. Visitors are greeted by the impressive, fully reconstructed form of a *Tyrannosaurus rex*, the terrifying meat-eater who measures up to forty-two feet in length. The T. rex is just one of the many species of dinosaur represented in the hall.

Even more notable than the T. rex for history buffs are the skeletal remains of *Hadrosaurus foulkii*. Found in nearby

---

Those interested in learning more about the Hadrosaurus foulkii and its discovery should take a ride over the Walt Whitman Bridge and head to Haddonfield, New Jersey, to see its birthplace. A life-size statue of the Hadrosaurus—sponsored by the Haddonfield Garden Club—is on display on Kings Highway.

Tyrannosaurus rex is still king of Dinosaur Hall at the Academy of Natural Sciences of Drexel University. More than thirty species of dinosaurs are featured in the hall. Photo: Will Klein

Haddonfield, New Jersey, in 1858, the *Hadrosaurus foulkii* was the first dinosaur skeleton ever displayed to the public—unveiled at the academy in 1868.

But for those who prefer their animals alive, the Butterflies! exhibit allows you to have a close encounter with these flying beauties from as far away as Africa and Southeast Asia—all while standing in a colorful garden. Little children can touch a tortoise or pet a snake in the Outside-In hands-on nature center, where the wonders of the great outdoors come inside to meet them. Live animals are also featured in museum presentations and shows throughout the day.

WHERE THE DINOSAURS ROAM

WHAT The Academy of Natural Sciences of Drexel University

WHERE 1900 Benjamin Franklin Pkwy., Philadelphia 19103

COST Adults, $17.95; children three to twelve, $13.95; seniors, $14.95; students and military (with ID), $14.95

PRO TIP Check your clothes before you leave! The last time we visited, my husband noticed that one of the butterflies from the Butterflies! exhibit was catching a ride on his shoulder. We returned the little hitchhiker to his tropical garden home inside the museum.

MYSTERIOUS AND KOOKY

Where is the Addams Family lurking in the City of Brotherly Love?

MYSTERIOUS AND KOOKY

WHAT The Charles Addams silhouettes and Kelly Family Gates

WHERE The Courtyard, Charles Addams Fine Arts Hall, 200 S. Thirty-Sixth St.

COST Free

PRO TIP Fans of the sixties TV series *The Addams Family* should also visit College Hall, the oldest building on the University of Pennsylvania's campus. It's said to be one of the inspirations for the creepy mansion that Gomez, Morticia, and family occupied in the series.

No worries . . . you won't find Lurch skulking inside Charles Addams Fine Arts Hall, home to the University of Pennsylvania's School of Design. But you will find plenty of references to Addams, creator of the *New Yorker* cartoon that inspired TV's *The Addams Family*, outside the building.

In a touch of whimsy Addams would admire, silhouettes of the fictional Addams family are now located outside the building. The piece, designed by Penn faculty member Lindsay Falck for the building's dedication, depicts eight members of the creepy clan. Trivia buffs should try to ID family matriarch Morticia; her husband, Gomez; offspring Wednesday and Pugsley; butler Lurch; and extended family members Grandmama, Uncle Fester, and Cousin Itt.

Nearby, find the Kelly Family Gates, which each display twenty-seven individual hands, some using tools commonly utilized in painting, sculpture, drawing, and manipulating clay. These hands are, obviously, a nod to Thing, the detached hand character who answered the phone and did other chores "handily" for the Addamses.

The members of the Addams family welcome visitors to Charles Addams Fine Arts Hall, home of the University of Pennsylvania's School of Design. ©Scott Lebeau

Point of interest: The gate was designed by Penn alum and sculptor Mark Lueders, who used the hands of fellow artists and faculty members to cast those on the gate.

Cartoonist Addams studied architecture at the U of P in the thirties. The Fine Arts Hall—formerly known as the Skinner Building—was renamed in his honor in 2001.

Originally a Jersey boy, Charles Addams came to the University of Pennsylvania after studying at Colgate for a year. He began submitting cartoons to the New Yorker in the early 1930s, and his cartoons were published regularly in the magazine until his death in 1988. He and his third wife, Marilyn Matthews "Tee" Miller, reportedly met in a pet cemetery. They called their New York estate "The Swamp."

³CELEBRATING AUDACIOUS FREEDOM

What major US city was the first to have an institution dedicated to the life and work of African Americans?

When the country celebrated its bicentennial in 1976, all eyes were on Philadelphia, the birthplace of the nation. Anticipating the attention, numerous updates and changes were made in the city, including moving the Liberty Bell to a new pavilion, refurbishing many historic buildings on an expanded Independence Mall, and opening several new museums.

One of these museums was the African American Historical and Cultural Museum, now known as the African American Museum in Philadelphia. Funded and built by the city itself, the museum tells the story of African American experience through its exhibits, interactive displays, artifacts, videos, and other technology.

The centerpiece of the museum is its permanent exhibit titled Audacious Freedom: African Americans in Philadelphia

---

Right outside the entrance to the museum, you'll find the compelling sculpture called Whispering Bells of Freedom: A Tribute to Crispus Attucks. Consisting of thirteen bells without clappers, representing the thirteen colonies, the sculpture reminds visitors that freedom didn't ring as loudly for some as for others. The sculpture provides a contrast to the Liberty Bell, just a few blocks away.

PHILADELPHIA
Conversations The people you're about to meet lived in Philadelphia during a period of enormous change. They fought for their freedom, accomplishing significant milestones that forced recognition of their rights. These people represent countless others whose untold stories make up the tapestry of present-day Philadelphia. They risked their lives because they believed in themselves, their community, and the great promise of this country.

Opened for the bicentennial celebration of 1976, the African American Museum features an interactive timeline detailing African American experiences following the Revolutionary War. Photo courtesy the African American Museum in Philadelphia.

1776–1876. The exhibit includes a narrated, interactive timeline that details the heritage and culture of African Americans in Philadelphia during our country's first century.

Visitors to the exhibit will encounter ten full-sized video projections of such torchbearers as Octavius Catto, the black educator and civil rights activist who was martyred in Philly, and civil rights activist and poet Frances Ellen Watkins Harper. Through the stories of these trailblazers, visitors receive a fuller understanding of the struggles and successes of the city's African American population during that crucial era.

CELEBRATING AUDACIOUS FREEDOM

WHAT African American Museum in Philadelphia, the country's first museum dedicated to the life and work of African Americans

WHERE 701 Arch St., Philadelphia 19106

COST Adults, $14; children four to twelve, seniors, and students with ID, $10

PRO TIP After learning about Octavius Catto at the museum, head over to City Hall to see the statue honoring him. Unveiled in 2017, it is Philly's first public statue honoring a specific African American.

<u>4</u> THE THINKING PERSON'S MUSEUM

How did Ben Franklin define useful knowledge?

Among the many historical sites on the Independence Mall, you can find the country's first successful public museum, national library, and academy of science—all under one roof.

Founded by Ben Franklin (who else?) in 1743, the American Philosophical Society was the country's first learned society, built for the purpose of "promoting useful knowledge." The society maintains this mission even today, supporting research and discovery, honoring notable accomplishments, and serving as a resource for scholars, especially through its extensive library. The society's Philosophical Hall—now a museum—was designated a National Historic Landmark in 1965.

The library contains an amazing array of historical documents and manuscripts, including a handwritten copy of the Declaration of Independence and journals kept by Lewis and Clark. Other notables include first editions of many books, including Charles Darwin's *On the Origin of Species*. A selection of the library's holdings is usually on display in the lobby for the public to see.

The Philosophical Society was founded two years after the University of Pennsylvania. Its original name was the American Philosophical Society Held at Philadelphia for Promoting Useful Knowledge. Ben Franklin was elected the society's first president.

CURIOUS
REVOLUTIONARIES
The Peales of Philadelphia

Rotating exhibitions are the mainstay at the American Philosophical Society, founded by Benjamin Franklin in 1743. The society's renowned collection traces American history and science from the early colonies to the modern day. Photo courtesy the American Philosophical Society.

THE THINKING PERSON'S MUSEUM

WHAT The American Philosophical Society

WHERE 104 S. Fifth St., Philadelphia 19106

COST Free. A $2 donation is requested. Guided tours are available, but advance reservations are necessary.

PRO TIP Go often. The museum is a rotating gallery that shows a different exhibition every year, centered around a theme inspired by the society's collections and history.

Most visitors, however, head to the museum, which has no real "permanent" exhibit but instead features different items from the society's vast collection. This virtual treasure trove of historical, artistic, and scientific information dates back to the Founding Fathers and reaches into the future. Memorable items include an early-eighteenth-century sundial; portraits of the Founding Fathers by Charles Willson Peale, Thomas Sully, and Gilbert Stuart; Thomas Jefferson's polygraph machine; and David Rittenhouse's telescope.

RECOLLECTIONS

Where is there a 100,000-square-foot memory box?

Imagine an attic where all your childhood treasures have been tucked away. And not only your own toys, decorations, and other cherished memorabilia, but those of your parents and your children, as well.

Well, stop imagining and get on board the tram ride through the Toy Box at the American Treasure Tour. Housed in an old B.F. Goodrich tire factory is an extensive assortment of childhood memories—from a miniature three-ring circus to a wall of Collegeville Halloween masks, and from a full-size Snow White with all seven dwarves to a variety of Happy Meal toys. All these and so much more are from the collection of a private, anonymous owner who shares them with visitors to the museum (much to the delight of those of us who, perhaps, have lost our own childhood favorites to the elements or adulthood).

Where else can you find a complete miniature three-ring circus, with concession stands and sideshow? Or listen to music ring out from Sadie Mae, the pink Wurlitzer Band Organ? Or ponder a castle made of 396,000 Popsicle sticks? Everywhere you look, you'll discover another treasure; every ride through, you'll find something you missed before.

Car lovers take note! Vintage cars and trucks—including a 1922 Stanley Steamer and a 1905 Franklin—are a highlight of the American Treasure Tour. For the most part, these cars are preserved, not restored, and most are still working!

The pink Wurlitzer Band Organ known as Sadie Mae still plays merrily as the tram tours pass by at the American Treasure Tour. ©Mary Dixon Lebeau

RECOLLECTIONS

WHAT American Treasure Tour, a pop culture museum and guided tram tour

WHERE One American Treasure Way, 422 Business Center, Oaks, PA 19456

COST Adults, $12.50; children, three to twelve, $5; children under three, free

PRO TIP The American Treasure Tour is open to the public Thursday through Saturday. The guided tram tour is included in your admission.

Another twenty thousand square feet is dedicated to the Music Room, full of auditory treats that delight the other senses, as well. The walls are bright with old album art and celebrity posters, while the aisles throughout the room feature immense dollhouses and dioramas. But the big attraction is the musical instruments and music makers, including hundreds of automatic music machines. Favorites include the Seeburg Style R Pipe-Organ Orchestra Photo Player, which once provided sound effects for silent films, and the Wurlitzer Mandolin PianOrchestra, with its peacock-shaped "wonder light."

Also a treasure: the small but knowledgeable staff, who provide impromptu demonstrations and give tours both educational and entertaining.

FARMER IN THE DEL-PHIA

Can you teach an old gardener new tricks?

For an old planting ground, Bartram's Garden is certainly forward-focused.

The grounds, which include John Bartram's house, a historic botanical garden, and an arboretum, cover forty-five acres on the west bank of the Schuylkill River. Horticulture and history live side by side on these grounds, home of some of the country's first gardens.

Quaker John Bartram owned this farm in the eighteenth century, building the original stone house and its additions through the years. The garden was planted in 1728; a greenhouse was added in 1760. Bartram devoted his life to the exploration and discovery of new North American species of plants; his garden once boasted the most varied collection of North American plants in the world. He has been credited for identifying more than two hundred native plants.

Today, visitors can enjoy the living collection, including the garden's signature tree, the *Franklinia alatamaha*, discovered by Bartram and his son William in 1765 and named for John's close friend, Ben Franklin. (But of course!) There are also ball fields, picnic areas, a boat dock, and a playground—as well as awe-inspiring views of the Philly skyline.

John Bartram planted his family here the same year he planted his garden—1728. The stone house on the grounds was built in stages over forty years. The house and the grounds were dedicated as National Historic Landmarks in 1963.

The Sankofa Community Farm is now fully rooted at Bartram's Gardens in Southwest Philly. The farm has increased access to fresh fruits and vegetables for people in the area. ©Scott Lebeau

FARMER IN THE DEL-PHIA

WHAT The Sankofa Community Farm and Bartram's Garden, a working farm teaching self-reliance on the grounds of the oldest surviving botanic garden in the country.

WHERE Fifty-Fourth Street and Lindbergh Boulevard, Philadelphia 19143

COST Visiting the grounds and the farm is free. There are two tours, one of the house and one of the garden, each of which costs $12 for adults and $10 for seniors and youth.

PRO TIP The Bartram House, a National Historic Landmark, is open for tours from April through October.

Equally awe-inspiring is a newer addition to the site—the Sankofa Community Farm at Bartram's Garden. Sankofa means "go back and get it" in the Twi language of modern-day Ghana, and the farm is committed to the practice of natural agriculture in Southwest Philly. Its mission is to help the people of the area build relationships with food, the land, and each other, while growing in spiritual awareness and connecting to the community's deep African Diaspora culture. Approximately twenty area high school students are hired to tend the farm each year, helping to distribute 15,000 pounds of fresh produce.

IT'S ELECTRIC!

Can a bust of Ben Franklin hold the key to community?

Almost every American schoolchild knows the story of how old Benjamin Franklin flew a kite out in the rain and discovered electricity. The secret of his success? He tied a key to the kite string, hoping to attract lightning that occurred during the thunderstorm. So, using keys to build a nine-foot-tall bronze bust of Philly's favorite Founding Father just seemed to make sense.

Located a block east of his grave, the bust of Franklin is the work of artist James Peniston—with the help of Philadelphia's elementary schoolchildren. After the artist visited Philly classrooms in 2005 and 2006, the kids donated more than one thousand old, unused keys from home. The kids also pitched in more than 1.8 million pennies that local firefighters collected to fund the artwork.

Casts of the keys were incorporated in the bust's exterior—but that's not the only secret hidden in the bust. At the first pouring of bronze for the sculpture, several Philly firefighters threw brass nameplates of fallen comrades into the melting metal. Both the children and the firefighters will be part of the statue forever—fitting for a bust called *Keys to Community.*

Girard Fountain Park is located on grounds where, in 1750, the Philadelphia Academy stood. Established with Franklin's help, it was at the time the city's largest building. The park is now maintained—perhaps fittingly—by the fire department.

A close-up view of some of the thousand keys donated by Philadelphia schoolchildren and used in the sculpture's texturing. The sculpture was partially funded by the city's fire department. ©Scott Lebeau

Inset: Sculptor James Peniston's Keys to Community *was dedicated October 5, 2007. It replaced the beloved* Penny Benny *by sculptor Reginald E. Beauchamp. ©Mary Dixon Lebeau*

IT'S ELECTRIC!

WHAT The Benjamin Franklin bust of keys, called *Keys to Community*

WHERE Girard Fountain Park, Fourth and Arch streets, Philadelphia 19106

COST Free

PRO TIP Numerous other destinations commemorating Franklin are within walking distance, including Franklin's gravesite, which is usually covered in pennies left by schoolchildren.

The bust, which stands on a five-foot, six-inch brick base, was commissioned and is owned by the city. It replaced the popular but deteriorating *Penny Franklin* sculpture, a six-foot acrylic bust of Franklin that was covered by pennies donated by schoolchildren.

ROW, ROW, ROW YOUR BOAT

Where's a great place to take a walk and enjoy the view?

First of all, a pronunciation lesson. The name of that river running west to east through the city? It's the Schuylkill, and it's pronounced SKOOL-kill. You may hear variations, but the emphasis is always on the first syllable. It shares its name with a major city roadway, the Schuylkill Expressway. The calm Schuylkill River is perfect for the activities of area rowers, from the unexperienced newcomer to the most competitive teams.

Boathouse Row is a series of twelve historic boating clubhouses that line the east bank of the Schuylkill River. Each boathouse is more than a century old and is the home base for a social and rowing club. The first, Lloyd Hall, is the recreation center of Fairmount Park. The next ten belong to rowing clubs. Each is a member of the Schuylkill Navy of

ROW, ROW, ROW YOUR BOAT

WHAT Boathouse Row, historic boating clubs and hub of activities

WHERE 1 Boathouse Row, Philadelphia 19130

COST Free

PRO TIP To get up close and personal, walk or run down Boathouse Row. But to see the real beauty of the houses, try walking down Martin Luther King Jr. Drive and viewing Boathouse Row from across the Schuylkill.

The Sedgeley Club operates the Lighthouse on Turtle Rock, built just west of Boathouse Row in 1887 to guide rowers and boaters on the Schuylkill.

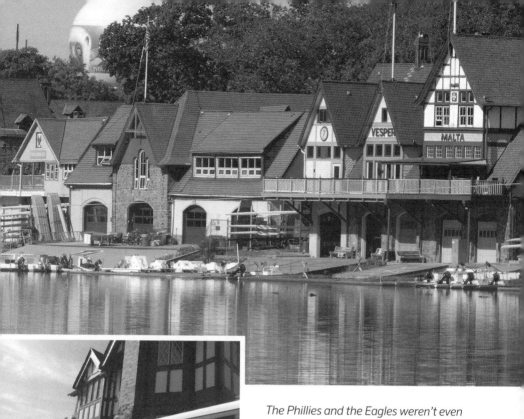

The Phillies and the Eagles weren't even around when rowing was the sport of the city in the mid-1800s. The first official club was the Bachelors Barge Club, founded in 1853. Members lost voting rights when they married. ©Scott Lebeau

Inset: Equipment outside a clubhouse on Boathouse Row. ©Scott Lebeau

Philadelphia, founded as a governing body for the activities of amateur rowers in 1858. The final building is the Sedgeley Club, a private social club.

Boathouse Row plays host to two annual globally recognized regattas, the Dad Vail Regatta and the Stotesbury Cup Regatta. But the area is alive with activity all year long. Joggers, dog-walkers, runners, and parents pushing strollers fill the sidewalks of Kelly Drive next to the clubhouses.

Known almost as much for their beauty as for their rowing activities, the iconic Victorian structures of Boathouse Row are outlined with lights year-round, with reflections that dance across the waters of the Schuylkill.

⁹ FREEDOM'S FIRST ADDRESS

Where did the First Continental Congress meet?

The Second Continental Congress most frequently convened at the Pennsylvania State House. In the summer of 1776, brave leaders met there to declare the colonies' independence from British rule. Eleven years (and a Revolutionary War) later, representatives met in the same place—the building now known as Independence Hall—to create, mold, and eventually sign our Constitution.

But where did the First Continental Congress meet? Well, here's a bit of a secret: The delegates from twelve colonies first met in what was—and still is—basically a union hall. Carpenters' Hall was the headquarters of the Carpenters' Company, a trade guild still meeting regularly today, that was fashioned like those of eighteenth-century England. When the First Continental Congress convened in 1774, many were concerned that British sympathizers were gathering at the Pennsylvania State House. The representatives—including George Washington, Benjamin Franklin, Roger Sherman, Samuel Adams, and Patrick Henry—chose to meet at Carpenters' Hall instead. It was here that they voted to support a trade embargo against Britain, which was the act that started the Revolutionary War.

Inside Carpenters' Hall, you'll find the delegates' chairs and an original banner carried in the Constitutional parade of 1788, as well as a scale model demonstrating methods used in the hall's construction.

Carpenters' Hall has been continuously owned and operated by the Carpenters' Company of the City and County of Philadelphia since 1770. It is the country's oldest craft guild. ©Scott Lebeau

Inset: Carpenters' Hall has been the setting for a variety of events throughout our history. Of course, it is most remembered as the site of the First Continental Congress in 1774, but it also hosted, at one time or another, the First and Second Banks of the United States, Franklin's Library Company, and the American Philosophical Society. ©Mary Dixon Lebeau

FREEDOM'S FIRST ADDRESS

WHAT Carpenters' Hall, the meeting place of the First Continental Congress

WHERE 320 Chestnut St., Philadelphia 19106

COST Free

PRO TIP Carpenters' Hall is closed Mondays year-round. It is also closed on Tuesdays in February. Independence Hall is open every day but Christmas.

Of course, not everyone was "all in" when it came to breaking away from England. Delegates on both sides of the issue met at Carpenters' Hall to debate. After seven weeks, the First Continental Congress drafted a declaration of colonial rights, detailing the desired relationship between the colonies and England. The delegates also agreed to meet again in May 1775 if their concerns were not addressed. It was at the subsequent meeting—right down the street, at Independence Hall—that the Founding Fathers drafted the Declaration of Independence.

10 IT'S THE END OF THE WORLD AS WE KNOW IT

Where did the country's first doomsday cult plan to wait it out?

Here's a secret that comes with a disclaimer: There are some who dismiss this story, suspecting that the structured hole in the hill is actually just a springhouse. Perhaps so. But if you're willing to suspend that logic, follow the trail into the woods . . . and remember, the hermit is watching!

From early on, Philadelphia had a reputation for religious tolerance, which made it the perfect place for German mystic and musician Johannes Kelpius and his followers. Known as "Hermits of the Wissahickon" or "The Society of the Woman in the Wilderness," this group settled in the remote area around Wissahickon Creek in 1694. There they planned to wait out the end of days, as they believed Kelpius's prediction that the world would end and Jesus would return that year.

IT'S THE END OF THE WORLD AS WE KNOW IT

WHAT Cave of Kelpius, supposedly the hiding place of a seventeenth-century doomsday cult

WHERE 777-795 Hermit Ln., Philadelphia 19128

COST Free

PRO TIP Keep your eyes open. Although the cave is marked, many just stumble upon it as they run, jog, or bike through the area.

The cave used to include a fireplace and chimney, but these structures—which suggest that this was more than a mere springhouse— were removed because of vandalism.

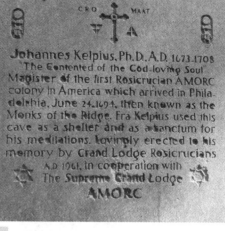

CRO ✝ MAAT

Johannes Kelpius, Ph.D. A.D. 1673-1708
The Contented of the God-loving Soul
Magister of the first Rosicrucian AMORC
colony in America which arrived in Phila-
delphia, June 24.1694, then known as the
Monks of the Ridge. Fra Kelpius used this
cave as a shelter and as a sanctum for
his meditations. Lovingly erected to his
memory by Grand Lodge Rosicrucians
A.D. 1961, in cooperation with
The Supreme Grand Lodge
AMORC

Many people stumble upon the Cave of Kelpius while taking a run through Wissahickon Valley Park. ©Scott Lebeau

Inset: A marker at the cave commemorates Johannes Kelpius, "contented of the God-loving soul." ©Scott Lebeau

Obviously, that didn't happen, but the cult—consisting solely of men—continued to live in the area, meditating and holding out hope for the end. The "Hermits" disbanded after Kelpius's death in 1708. But many believed that the enlarged cave off the current Wissahickon bike trail was once the hiding spot of the cult, the cavern they were going to hide in as the end times played out.

Finding the site is a bit of a challenge—and that's part of the fun. You have to travel a short distance off Hermit Lane through the woods, stepping over fallen trees and hiking up and down some steep, hilly areas. The farther you go into the woods, the easier it becomes to forget you're still in Philadelphia, as all the sounds of the city disappear. But not to worry—the city is still out there, and life goes on.

<u>11</u> DEATH AND TAXES

Where does Ben Franklin RIP (rest in pennies)?

Some people die at twenty-five and aren't buried until seventy-five.—Benjamin Franklin

It may not be a secret, but it may be surprising to learn that Ben Franklin, the person most closely connected with the City of Brotherly Love (sorry, Rocky!), was actually born in Massachusetts. He grew up in Beantown, but after a fallout with a family member, he ran away to Philly, and the rest is, well, history.

Franklin's fingerprints are all over this fair city. From the institute bearing his name to the hospital he founded, from the parkway to the library and even to the prison, Benjamin Franklin is everywhere you look. But the truth is, there's only one place to really find old Ben in Philly—and that's at Christ Church Burial Ground, where the body of the inventor/politician/scribe is resting.

Christ Church Burial Ground, blocks away from the church

DEATH AND TAXES

WHAT Christ Church Burial Ground, site of Ben Franklin's grave

WHERE 340 N. Fifth St., Philadelphia 19106

COST Adults, $3; children, $1. Guided tours are available for an additional cost.

PRO TIP Because of weather, the burial grounds are closed in January and February.

The Franklin family plot is in the corner of the cemetery, easily visible from the street. If you're visiting, bring pennies. It's traditional to leave a penny on Franklin's grave, an homage to his belief that "a penny saved is a penny earned."

The Body of
B. Franklin, Printer,
ike the Cover of an old Book,
Its Contents torn out,
d Stript of its Lettering & Gilding,
Lies here, Food for Worms.
ut the Work shall not be lost,
For it will as he believ'd
appear once more
a new and more elegant Edition
Corrected and improved
By the Author.

(This epitaph written by Franklin as a young
man, was not intended to be used. His nearby
gravestone was prepared in exact accordance
with the instructions contained in his will.)

This gravesite restored
by the Poor Richard Club
of Philadelphia
through the generosity
of Howard C. Story
in memory of his parents
ward A. and Mary Elizabeth Story

Remembering that "a penny saved is a penny earned," visitors to Benjamin Franklin's grave leave pennies on his grave. ©Mary Dixon Lebeau

Inset: Despite all his accomplishments, Benjamin Franklin—always the humble Quaker—identified himself as a printer, as noted in the inscription he wrote that appears on a plaque at Christ Church. ©Scott Lebeau

itself, consists of fourteen hundred grave markers on some four thousand graves, all situated on two beautiful acres of land. Here you'll find the final resting place of many Colonial-era notables, including Dr. Benjamin Rush, who signed the Declaration of Independence and founded Fairleigh Dickinson College; George Ross, Betsy's uncle, who also signed the Declaration; John Dunlap, printer of the first daily newspaper; and Dr. William Camac, founder of the Philadelphia Zoo, the nation's first.

Many of the stones are showing their age, worn down by the elements through the centuries. Some plots are identified with markers where the inscriptions are no longer readable. But the Franklin family plot has been recently restored. The marble grave marker reads simply, "Benjamin and Deborah Franklin 1790."

<u>12</u> *HUMANITY IN MOTION*

Where can you spot the city's most sure-footed residents?

Look! Up in the sky! It's a bird . . . it's a plane . . . it's *Humanity in Motion*!

Currently the tallest building in the city, the fifty-eight-story Comcast Center is the headquarters of the Comcast Corporation. Although its main function is as an office building, it has been a go-to attraction for residents and visitors alike since it opened in 2008.

The stunning *Comcast Experience*, a two-thousand-square-foot video wall in the main lobby, amazes audiences with its visual clarity, beauty, and creativity. Below the lobby, the Market at Comcast Center tempts with its popular eateries, specialty food, and retail shopping. Events such as craft demonstrations and food samplings are held periodically in the market.

All these aspects make the Comcast Center a very special office space—but they are very well known and extremely popular. So what makes this a secret? Shhh . . . look up.

It's easy to miss the beam walkers if your eyes are on the ground. Look up and see Humanity in Motion at the Comcast Center. Just to keep things grounded, a father and son are part of the artwork—and part of the audience—in the Comcast Center. ©Scott Lebeau

As you enter the Comcast Center through the 140-foot glass atrium, you'll see what appear to be people walking across the beams of the building. This is *Humanity in Motion*, a sculpture by world-renowned artist Jonathan Borofsky. Ten horizontal poles (or beams) span the eight-story "winter garden" at various levels, each holding a life-size figure frozen "in motion." Two other figures—a father and son—stand at ground level, gazing up in wonder at the activity above.

The building itself is also a piece of art, wrapped in a "glass curtain," an energy-saving mirror-like exterior that allows for a panoramic view of the city around it.

The building is gorgeous, but looks aren't everything. The Comcast Center has earned LEED (Leadership in Energy and Environmental Design) gold status and is currently the tallest LEED-certified building in the country. Among its many energy-saving features is an underground parking lot, which eliminates exposed heat-absorbing asphalt.

DREAM COME TRUE

What piece of art did Philadelphians fight to keep?

Built in 1910, the Curtis Center building was originally the headquarters of the Curtis Publishing Company. Publisher Cyrus H. K. Curtis founded the company in 1891, following his success with such publications as *Ladies' Home Journal* and the *Saturday Evening Post*. The publications were sold mid-century, and the building is now being refurbished as office space, with its grand atrium a popular wedding venue.

But the jewel in the crown of this historic building is almost hidden away behind the atrium's waterfall. In the marble lobby is a twenty-four-panel Tiffany mosaic made of handblown, handcrafted glass. This is *Dream Garden*, an imaginary garden of color and light.

The mosaic was designed by Philadelphia artist Maxfield Parrish, then manufactured and installed by the Louis Comfort Tiffany Studios in 1916, one of only three such works the company undertook. The landscape was created using more than 100,000 pieces of favrile (Old Saxon for "handmade") glass in 260 different colors. It took six months and countless manhours to install the fifteen-by-forty-nine-foot mosaic.

Louis Comfort Tiffany created an iridescent sheen on glass through a unique process of exposing it to the fumes of molten metals. It took an estimated thirty craftsmen more than a year to handcraft the mosaic, blowing, cutting, painting, and assembling the glass.

The iridescent sheen on the glass of this one-of-a-kind mosaic gives the landscape a dreamy effect. ©Mary Dixon Lebeau

But the city almost lost its surreal landscape. In 1998, casino mogul Steve Wynn planned to purchase the mosaic and move it to his Atlantic City casino. A citywide protest ensued, and the plans were dropped. The Pew Charitable Trusts provided $3.5 million to the Pennsylvania Academy of the Fine Arts to purchase the mosaic. It has since been given the designation of "historic object" under the city's Historic Preservation Ordinance.

DREAM COME TRUE

WHAT *Dream Garden* mural at the Curtis Center, a one-of-a-kind glass mosaic in a historic building

WHERE 601 Walnut St., Philadelphia 19106

COST Free

PRO TIP The Curtis Center is just across the street from Washington Square, steps away from the back entrance of Independence Hall. Park on the street here when visiting any or all three. The lobby is not open on Sundays or holidays.

WE HOLD THESE TRUTHS TO BE SELF-EVIDENT

Where was the Declaration of Independence penned?

The two-story Georgian-style brick house on the southwest corner of Seventh and Market streets is simple and unassuming. But it is on this site that one of the Founding Fathers penned the rousing words that set the colonies moving toward independence.

The house was built in 1775 by Jacob Graff Jr., a well-known Philadelphia bricklayer. The following year, Graff rented two of the rooms on the second floor to a thirty-three-year-old Virginian named Thomas Jefferson—and secured the Graff House's place in history. At the time, Jefferson was a delegate to the Continental

WE HOLD THESE TRUTHS TO BE SELF-EVIDENT

WHAT Declaration (Graff) House, historical site where the Declaration of Independence was written

WHERE Seventh and Market streets, Philadelphia 19103

COST Free

PRO TIP The house is open seasonally. Best to check the Independence National Historical Park website or call the Visitor Center for hours.

On the back of the Declaration of Independence, there is a message stating, "Original Declaration of Independence dated 4th July 1776." Experts believe it was a label added at a later date. Despite the plot point in the movie *National Treasure*, there is no secret message on the back.

The words of the Declaration of Independence, declaring our right to life, liberty, and the pursuit of happiness, are emblazoned on the Declaration House. The house is unassuming, simple brick, a throwback between skyscrapers. But it is here that the words that declared our country's independence were penned. ©Scott Lebeau

Congress. He believed the time had come for the colonies to break ties with England—and he was selected to pen the words that would announce this decision to the world. Using the Virginia Constitution as a template, Jefferson took approximately three weeks to write the document.

After editing by his fellow delegates to the Second Continental Congress in 1776, the Declaration of Independence announcing that the colonies declared themselves free of British rule was adopted, and a new nation was born on July 4, 1776. Jefferson's original draft, with changes by Ben Franklin and John Adams penned in, is now preserved in the Library of Congress.

The original Graff House was torn down in 1883, but it was rebuilt in 1975 on the original site by the National Park Service, staying true to photographs of the original. Visitors to the site now can view a short film about the writing of the Declaration, as well as other exhibits, on the first floor. Venture up to the second floor, where Jefferson's bedroom and parlor have been re-created using period furnishings and reproductions.

<u>15</u> WHAT NERVE!

Who is Drexel University's longest-serving employee?

When I first met Harriet, I thought she was an artistic interpretation, a macramé of sorts. But what looks like string art is an actual bundle of nerves—the human nervous system, dissected from the body and on display at the Drexel University College of Medicine.

WHAT NERVE!

WHAT Harriet Cole at Drexel University College of Medicine, a display of the human nervous system

WHERE 2900 W. Queen Ln., Philadelphia 19129

COST Free

PRO TIP You can find Harriet and the other exhibits right outside the Barnes & Noble located on the lower floor of the college.

This is Harriet Cole—or what remains of her. Legend has it that, in the late nineteenth century, Cole was employed as a cleaner at the school (then Hahnemann Medical College). Among the classrooms she cleaned was the room where Dr. Rufus B. Weaver dissected cadavers with the medical students. How Cole knew Weaver, a professor of anatomy and 1865 Penn Medical College grad, is lost to history.

Weaver had a specific use in mind for Harriet's remains. In what was a medical first, he dissected and mounted

In nearby display cases, you can find the Geckeler Collection, casts of the circulatory systems of the heart, kidney, and lungs, prepared by Dr. George D. Geckeler, the first director of Hahnemann's pioneer Cardiovascular Research Institute.

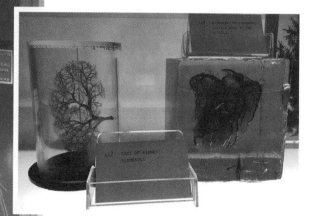

It may look like a bizarre macramé project, but the nervous system of Harriet Cole was an award-winning teaching tool used in medical schools and textbooks. ©Scott Lebeau

Inset: The Geckeler Collection at Drexel University College of Medicine includes casts of the heart, kidneys, and lungs. You can see the collection in a display case near Harriet. ©Mary Dixon Lebeau

Harriet's complete nervous system to be used as a teaching aid. The dissection took a full five months of eight- to ten-hour days, as the doctor painstakingly removed all flesh and bone from the nerves before coating them and mounting them in a roughly human shape.

Through the years, Harriet has taught medical students across the country about the nervous system. The mounted system has appeared in textbooks, doctors' offices, laboratories, and classrooms throughout the country. In 1893, she appeared at the World's Columbian Exposition in Chicago, winning an Exhibition Medal and a blue ribbon for Weaver's work. She was also the subject of a *Time* magazine article in the thirties and a *Life* magazine photo essay in 1960.

No longer used as a part of the curriculum, Harriet stands watch in the Student Activities Center at the Drexel University College of Medicine.

What was once the country's most expensive building– and Philly's scariest?

The gargoyles still stand sentry on the outside of Eastern State Penitentiary, chains binding them to the gray stone walls, snarls on their faces warning visitors of the desolation within. The doors of this Gothic-inspired prison, at the time both the most famous and most expensive in the world, first opened in 1829. Visitors worldwide came to see the building, which was then state of the art, having central heat and running water even before the White House did.

Its architecture is breathtaking, a dark fortress designed to embody the definition of "penitentiary," bringing prisoners to a point of penitence or regret, as well as punishing them. This was accomplished through a system of isolation. Inmates never came in contact with one another; each had his own cell where he remained twenty-three hours a day. Even when leaving the cell, he would go to a separate courtyard, his head covered with a black cloth to avoid human contact. The use of isolation as a correctional method became known as the Pennsylvania System. It had numerous critics (including Charles Dickens) and was

The Philadelphia Society for Alleviating the Miseries of Public Prisons, the world's first prison reform group, was created by Dr. Benjamin Rush in 1787. An early member was none other than Benjamin Franklin. The group, which promotes social justice and prison reform, still exists as the Pennsylvania Prison Society.

The long, narrow hallways of Eastern State, where isolation was used to bring prisoners to a state of repentance.
©Mary Dixon Lebeau

ALCATRAZ OF THE EAST

WHAT Eastern State Penitentiary

WHERE 2027 Fairmount Ave., Philadelphia 19130

COST At the door, tickets are $16 for adults, $14 for seniors, and $12 for students and children 7–12. You can save $2 off each ticket by purchasing in advance online. The tour is not recommended for children under the age of seven.

PRO TIP The fright bar is raised to a new high every fall as Halloween approaches. Prisoners—or their ghosts—return to Eastern in the area's most frightening haunted experience, *Terror Behind Walls*. If you dare, visit during the spirit season to see cells come alive again—at an additional cost.

officially abandoned at Eastern State in 1913.

Through the years, the prison housed some of America's most notorious criminals. Best known is probably Al Capone, arrested in Philly in 1929 for carrying an unlicensed revolver. The Chicago gangster spent eight months here, in a lavish cell featuring oriental rugs, plush furniture, and a radio.

Capone's cell in its restored state is just one of the fascinating stops on the audio tour at Eastern State Penitentiary. The prison officially closed in January 1970. Today, it opens daily for tours of the historic building. The audio tour features ten stops on the main route, with an additional forty-seven available to visitors, who can design their own tour based on their interests.

FALL OF THE HOUSE OF EDGAR

Did one of America's most celebrated poets—and his haunting bird—roost in Philly?

Quoth the raven—well, why yes, Edgar Allan Poe did live six years of his mysterious short life right in Philadelphia. And you can visit his small home on Seventh Street—now a National Historic Site—where he, his wife, and his mother-in-law spent the last year or so of that time. It's where Poe was perhaps his most productive, at a time when he fought some of his most frightening demons.

A visit starts with a short film about Poe, his works, and his time in Philly. Then visitors can go on a self-guided tour of the three-story house and cellar, which is reminiscent of the basement in Poe's short story "The Black Cat." (Yes, it is speculated that he wrote the story here.) We enjoyed playing with the eerie word magnets on the upper floor—a latter-day addition, no doubt, but proof that poetry isn't as easy as it looks (or sounds). Guided tours are also available—and come with a special visual effect. Ask the ranger what beats beneath the loose floorboards on the upper floor.

After your tour, be sure to visit the Reading Room, where you can listen to Poe's poetry and short stories on CD. This room, unlike those in Poe's original house, is restored and furnished using nineteenth-century furniture—although, sadly, not Poe's. That has been lost to the ages and will be seen, well, "nevermore."

Another clue you're in the right place—a raven guards the courtyard of the Edgar Allan Poe National Historical Site. Could it be Grip (page 54)? ©Mary Dixon Lebeau

FALL OF THE HOUSE OF EDGAR

WHAT Edgar Allan Poe National Historical Site

WHERE 532 N. Seventh St., Philadelphia 19123

COST Free

PRO TIP Be sure to give your kids time to complete the Junior Ranger Program at the Poe House. They'll learn a lot about the master of scare and will come home with a neat—and free—souvenir, as well. Just ask one of the rangers in the Visitor Center for details.

The Edgar Allan Poe National Historic Site is part of the National Park Service. The property includes the actual Poe home, as well as two other buildings, previously residential, that were not built until after Poe left Philadelphia for New York. The original Poe home, a rental, can be explored in its decaying state—not much has been done by way of restoration to maintain the integrity of the building. The other buildings house the film area, the welcome area, a gift shop, and other exhibits.

Outside the building, a statue of a large black bird stands watch over the house and its visitors. Yes, it's the raven, representing one of Poe's most haunting works, the poem "The Raven."

18 THE STREET OF PHILADELPHIA

THE STREET OF PHILADELPHIA

WHAT Elfreth's Alley, the country's oldest continuously inhabited residential street

WHERE 124-126 Elfreth's Alley, Philadelphia 19106

COST $5 per person to visit the Museum House

PRO TIP This is a residential street, so remember, people actually live here! Please respect their privacy. If you'd like to see inside one of the homes, the Museum House is open from noon to five, Friday through Sunday.

Where can you find the oldest neighborhood in the United States?

Philadelphia is often called a city of neighborhoods. It seems ironic, then, that the oldest neighborhood in the country wasn't even on the original plans for the city.

Elfreth's Alley was originally a cart path that connected local artisans and tradesmen to the city and the ports on the Delaware River. Named after silversmith Jeremiah Elfreth, Elfreth's Alley first opened in 1706 and has served as a residential street since that time. Most of the original owners were tradespeople—dressmakers, butchers, shoemakers, bakers, and the like—who ran their businesses

Residents of Elfreth's Alley open their doors to visitors a few times each year. One of the most popular ticketed events is Deck the Alley, a day in early December when visitors can enjoy the homes—inside and out—in their holiday splendor.

Welcome to Elfreth's Alley
Our Nation's Oldest Residential Street

- Yes, people really do live here, and have continuously lived here since 1713

- 29 of the 32 houses are private homes, please enjoy your visit but respect the residents

- Our Museum house at no. 126 is furnished as it would have been in the 1760's

- Our house at no. 124 hosts pop-up exhibits, special programs and a selfie gallery with colonial costumes

- We are open to the public Friday, Saturday, and Sunday from 12-5 with additional seasonal hours.

Admission is $5 per person (family rate available)

For more information or to take a tour please stop by house no. 124

When you live on the oldest residential street in the country, you can expect tourists at your door. Visitors flock to Elfreth's Alley. Inset: A posted sign spells out the rules for visitors to Elfreth's Alley. Peeking into windows or walking in the front door is strictly prohibited.
©Scott Lebeau

out of the first floor of their homes.

The thirty-two brick rowhomes that currently make up the alley were built between the 1720s and the 1830s. The street itself is cobblestone and slate, with sidewalks of red brick. The quaint homes pay homage to the time when the Founding Fathers roamed these streets, with unique details such as the busybody mirror, a three-mirrored device hung from an upper floor to allow homeowners to see who was at the door without being seen themselves.

Two of the homes collectively make up the Museum House. These are open on extended weekends to visitors interested in seeing what the homes looked like during Colonial times. Inside you'll see period furnishings; old hearths; bunting, flags, and quilts; and other home décor in patriotic red, white, and blue.

WATER, WATER EVERYWHERE

How does water work?

History. Education. Science. Architecture. Imagination. Culture. All these things seem to come together at the Fairmount Water Works.

Philadelphia's most successful pumping station—the Fairmount Water Works—was built in response to the growing need for clean water by Philly's ever-increasing population. The city saw water delivery as a municipal responsibility and constructed the Water Works in 1815 and a huge outdoor reservoir (now the site of the Philadelphia Museum of Art) in 1820. The Water Works' engine house was designed with an eye to architectural beauty as well as engineering ingenuity, and the site was an international showcase for the city until it was decommissioned in 1909.

In the years that followed, the pumping equipment was removed and the building was used as an aquarium, then as a public swimming pool. Today, the building is restored and repurposed as an environmental education center focusing on the history and science of our watershed.

That may sound a bit, well, dry, but a visit to the Fairmount Water Works is anything but. Since it reopened as the Delaware River Basin's Official Watershed Education

A long-unused swimming pool can be found beneath the Water Works. This is the Kelly Natatorium, a converted aquarium-turned-public-pool funded by the Kelly family. It has been closed to the public since 1972 after being damaged by Hurricane Agnes.

As well as being a National Historic Landmark, the Fairmount Water Works has been recognized for the beauty and ingenuity of its design. ©Scott Lebeau Inset: Historical equipment, such as the water wheel and turbine, tell of the past of Fairmount Water Works. ©Mary Dixon Lebeau

WATER, WATER EVERYWHERE

WHAT Fairmount Water Works, historic site and interpretive center

WHERE 640 Waterworks Dr., Philadelphia 19130

COST Free

PRO TIP Two-hour free parking is available on Waterworks Drive, behind the Philadelphia Museum of Art. Open six days a week (Tuesday – Saturday, 10 a.m. – 5 p.m.; Sunday, 1 p.m. – 5 p.m.). Visit fairmountwaterworks.org for upcoming events and tours.

Center in 2003, the interpretive center has provided fun and fascinating hands-on activities and exhibits showcasing the importance of water in our world.

Visit the Engine House Theater to see an award-winning movie about the city's history and the role the Water Works played as Philly grew. Or check out the groundbreaking freshwater mussel hatchery and learn how these mollusks help clean our waterways. You'll gain a new understanding and appreciation for the water flowing from your tap.

What's the best way to clean up Dirty Franks?

Considering how essential he is to the history of both the city and the nation, it would be natural to think Ben Franklin is the only "Frank" to make a mark in Philadelphia.

Natural, but totally wrong.

If you head down to the corner of Pine and Thirteenth streets, you'll find a plethora of Franks gracing the exterior of Dirty Franks, a neighborhood bar that has become a Philly institution. Dirty Franks first opened its doors on November 8, 1933—less than a month prior to the repeal of Prohibition. Since December 1978, it has also been the home of the Off the Wall Gallery, an exhibit space for local painters, photographers, sculptors, and other artsy types.

You don't have to be a bar patron, however, to enjoy the art. The Washington Square West Civic Association wanted to brighten up the exterior of the corner property, so it requested the help of Mural Arts Philadelphia, the

The latest Frank to join the mural is Pope Francis, who was added along with former Philadelphia poet laureate Frank Sherlock in 2015, the year of the pope's visit to the city. Are you wondering what beloved Phillies pitcher Tug McGraw is doing up there? McGraw, known for pitching the final game when the Phillies won the 1980 World Series and for being country superstar Tim McGraw's father, was born Frank Edwin McGraw Jr. Now there's a secret!

From Aretha Franklin to Frank Zappa, there are Franks all around the block. Artist David McShane purposely didn't label the Franks, instead allowing viewers to guess. ©Mary Dixon Lebeau

largest public art program in the United States. Mural Arts takes on between fifty and one hundred projects a year; in April 2001, the *Famous Franks* mural was complete.

Visitors to the area have fun naming the Franks immortalized on the mural. Old Blue Eyes, Frank Sinatra, stares up at Frank Morgan, the actor portraying the Wizard of Oz. Frankenstein's monster appears next to FDR. You'll find both a frankfurter and chicken king Frank Perdue. Frank Burns from *MASH*, architect Frank Lloyd Wright, and St. Francis of Assisi all make appearances in this amusing mural.

LET'S FOLLOW THE MONEY AND SEE WHERE IT GOES

WHAT The Federal Reserve Bank's Money in Motion interactive exhibit about the history of American money

WHERE The Federal Reserve Bank of Philadelphia, 100 N. Sixth St., Philadelphia

COST Free

PRO TIP Because of the nature of the banking business, security here is ultra-tight. Be prepared for an airport-style security check; no photography is allowed inside the building.

How does money move?

The Philly Fed—or, more formally, the Federal Reserve Bank of Philadelphia—is one of twelve regional Federal Reserve Banks. Together with the Board of Governors, these banks make up the Federal Reserve System, which is charged with ensuring the security and strength of our country's economic system.

That all sounds pretty dry, but here's a secret: A visit to the Philly Fed is educational, interactive, and fun—and visitors walk away with a one-hundred-dollar souvenir.

To learn more, visitors can peruse the seventeen stations that make up the Fed's Money

The world's largest mobile, Alexander Calder's *White Cascade*, hangs from a skylight in the Fed. It is one of two pieces of art designed specifically for the Federal Reserve Bank of Philadelphia as part of the Philadelphia Redevelopment Authority's Percent for Art program

FEDERAL RESERVE BANK OF PHILADELPHIA

The mission of the Federal Reserve Bank is to create the financial conditions that foster economic growth. The Fed in Philly serves eastern Pennsylvania, southern New Jersey, and Delaware. Inset: Money past, present, and future—that's what Money in Motion is all about. The exhibit is a fun, interactive way to learn about the history of central banking in our country. ©Scott Lebeau

in Motion exhibit. First, you'll be greeted by Ben Franklin (yeah, he's everywhere!) as he comes to life on a one-hundred-dollar bill. Next, you can choose one of the interactive stations where you can read, take quizzes, play games— and, in the process, learn all about the history of money and the way it flows in our economy.

One station, titled Monitoring Monetary Policy, allows visitors to select a decade from the fifties through the nineties to learn how the economy fared at that time, using the economic indicators of the day. Other topics range from Early Money in America to more modern-day topics, such as identity theft protection and credit card fraud. Finally, the Fed looks at the future, as visitors make a transaction with a teller of the future in Payments 2200.

Fun fact: The vault at the Fed is the size of a football field and contains billions of dollars at any given time. While you're there, view a rare $100,000 bill, try to pick out counterfeit cash, and exchange one of your old quarters for a shiny new collector's version.

And even more fun, each visitor walks away with a free souvenir—a little bag containing approximately one hundred dollars in shredded money. Now, where else can you get money for nothing?

THE HOME OF THE BRAVE

Where can you relive the history of firefighting?

The country's first volunteer fire company, the Union Fire Company, was founded by—who else?—Benjamin Franklin, right here in Philadelphia in 1736. But the city's history with firefighting dates back even earlier than that. City founder William Penn—a witness to the Great Fire of London in 1666—planned for resisting fire in the city back in the late 1600s. (That was one reason so many of the buildings were brick.)

Today, those interested in the art of firefighting will enjoy visiting Fireman's Hall Museum: The National Fire House and Museum of Philadelphia. Founded in 1967, the museum is under the management of the city's fire department and was expanded for the bicentennial. The museum is located in Old City on the site of Engine Company Number 8's old fire house.

Some of the original artifacts used by members of that first company, including a hand pumper reportedly used by

---

THE HOME OF THE BRAVE

WHAT Fireman's Hall Museum: The National Fire House and Museum of Philadelphia

WHERE 147 N. Second St., Philadelphia 19106

COST Free, donations appreciated

PRO TIP The museum is open Tuesdays through Saturdays 10 a.m. – 4 p.m. Extended hours until 9 p.m. the first Friday of every month.

Fireman's Hall Museum is staffed by real firefighters, who are knowledgeable and always willing to discuss exhibits and answer questions.

"THE COWARD DIES A THOUSAND DEATHS, THE VALIANT DIE BUT ONE."

A stunning tribute to those firefighters who have protected the City of Brotherly Love through the centuries, this stained-glass window is a featured piece in Fireman's Hall Museum. Inset: Also breathtaking: the tribute to the heroic firefighters of 9/11, which includes genuine hoses, badges, and other memorabilia, as well as dirt taken from the site of the World Trade Center. ©Scott Lebeau

Franklin himself, are on display. Historical highlights include a 1730 engine, painted parade hats, a three-story brass fire pole, historic pictures, and old fire insurance policies. Interactive displays offer young visitors the opportunity to try on fire gear, steer fire boats, and play interactive educational computer games, including "When to Call 911." Video displays tell the story of the history of firefighting, including the Great Fire of 1839, when fifty-two buildings burned down in Philadelphia.

Upstairs, a beautiful stained-glass window showcases those heroes who gave their lives in fire rescue efforts in Philly. There's also a touching memorial tribute to the firefighters of September 11.

45

OLD MONEY

WHAT First Bank of the United States and Second Bank of the United States

WHERE First Bank of the United States, 116 S. Third St., Philadelphia 19112; Second Bank of the United States, 420 Chestnut St., Philadelphia 19106

COST Admission to the Second Bank of the United States and portrait gallery is free.

PRO TIP The Second Bank of the United States is open to the public on weekends only. The First Bank of the United States is not open to visitors.

Where did Alexander Hamilton leave his fingerprints on Philadelphia?

The Revolutionary War won the colonists their freedom from England, but it also left them in a lot of debt. Some states were on the verge of bankruptcy. Enter Secretary of the Treasury Alexander Hamilton, who proposed a plan for a national bank to handle the country's fiscal affairs. His proposal and the pushback that followed set the stage for the new country's financial system.

The First Bank of the United States opened in Carpenters' Hall in 1791, but it moved to its permanent home on Third Street six years later. The new bank headquarters was

An unusual and fascinating piece in the portrait gallery is the death mask of President George Washington. The artist, Charles Willson Peale, was a Revolutionary soldier who is also credited with helping establish the Philadelphia Museum, one of the country's first museums.

More than one hundred portraits by the famous painter Charles Willson Peale are displayed in the portrait gallery. ©Scott Lebeau

designed by architect Samuel Blodgett Jr. and is now considered the oldest building in America with a classical façade. The building's two-story portico boasts a proud bald eagle, which was named a national symbol just fourteen years before the bank's opening. The oldest bank building in America, it currently houses offices for the National Park Service.

Also located in Philadelphia, the Second Bank of the United States was similarly established in response to war debt—this time, the cost of the War of 1812. This bank was authorized by President James Madison in 1816. Like its predecessor, the Second Bank caused a political debate that in 1832 led to the election of anti-bank presidential candidate Andrew Jackson over pro-bank candidate Henry Clay. The bank closed four years later.

However, the building, modeled after the Greek Parthenon, now houses an extraordinary collection of eighteenth-century portraits by Charles Willson Peale, as well as paintings by other artists. Visitors to the gallery will find portraits of many of the most influential men of the early days of our country, including all the signers of the Declaration of Independence, Patrick Henry, the Marquis de Lafayette, and, of course, Alexander Hamilton.

<u>24</u> FRANKLIN'S FOUNDATION

Can you describe Ben Franklin in one word?

Printer. Publisher. Statesman. Inventor. Diplomat. Author. Postmaster.

All of these words, and so many more, can be used in a description of Benjamin Franklin. His fingerprints are all over the city of Philadelphia—but his footsteps can most easily be traced back here, to the Franklin Court area where he lived his final years.

Built in 1976 for the bicentennial celebration, Franklin Court was established on the very site where Ben Franklin lived from 1763 until his death in 1790. Because there were no records of what his three-story, ten-room home looked like, a fifty-four-foot-high steel "ghost structure" was constructed to show visitors the actual location and parameters of the house. A similar ghost structure recreates the print shop managed by Ben's grandson, Benjamin Franklin Bache. Franklin's home was razed in 1812, and only the actual foundation remains on site today, embedded in the ground.

But the ghost structures in the courtyard tell only part of Franklin's fascinating story. To hear the rest, head into the Benjamin Franklin Museum, also on site. There are five rooms, each dedicated to characteristics of old Ben—from

---

Benjamin Franklin had a fondness for squirrels, which were known as skuggs in Colonial times. While touring the museum, keep an eye out for squirrel figurines, as the squirrel is the museum mascot and appears throughout the building.

This reconstructed "ghost" house indicates the boundaries and size of the home Benjamin Franklin lived in from 1736 until his death in 1790. The ghost structure is made of square tubular steel. The actual house was razed in 1812. ©Scott Lebeau

rebellious to dutiful and from persuasive to curious. In each, interactive touchscreens, videos, and artifacts detail Franklin's history, his personality, and his contributions to our country.

Franklin Court also provides access to other Franklin-related sites, including the Franklin Court Printing Office, where National Park Rangers demonstrate how a daily newspaper was published in the eighteenth century using typesetting desks, drying racks, and hand-operated presses. There's also a B. Free Franklin Post Office, the only Colonial-themed office run by the United States Postal Service.

FRANKLIN'S FOUNDATION

WHAT Franklin Court, historic site of Ben Franklin's home and printing office; also a museum dedicated to Ben Franklin

WHERE 322 Market St., Philadelphia, and the immediate surroundings

COST Adults, $5; children four to sixteen, $2; children under three, free; courtyard and printing office are free

PRO TIP The gift shop at the Benjamin Franklin Museum may be the best place in the city for Ben Franklin souvenirs. The Fragments of Franklin Court exhibit, also part of Franklin Court, is open seasonally in warmer weather. Check the National Park Service website for times.

²⁵ BIG BEN

What exactly is an automaton?

Around here, almost everyone knows where to find the world's largest heart. Since 1953, the Franklin Institute has been home to the Giant Heart (originally called the *Engine of Life* exhibit). The walk-through heart is the proper size for a person 220 feet tall.

The heart, of course, is no secret. And neither is the Franklin Institute, one of the nation's oldest and most popular science museums. But despite its popularity, the Franklin Institute is keeping some secrets. You may know about SportsZone, the Train Factory, and the IMAX Theater, but did you ever visit Big Ben?

The Benjamin Franklin National Memorial is located in the rotunda of the Franklin Institute—and is free of charge to visit. A twenty-foot-high statue of the statesman/inventor is the showpiece of the room, which is fashioned after the Roman Pantheon. Visitors can watch a film about Franklin, *Benjamin Franklin Forever,* inside the memorial.

Another secret: Upstairs in the Amazing Machine exhibit, you can find an automaton with the largest memory of any such machine ever constructed.

The Franklin Institute has a plethora of artwork, information, and memorabilia about its namesake, Benjamin Franklin. Check out the various busts, commemorative medallions, and paintings. Exhibits also feature a bent lightning rod, his glass armonica (a musical instrument he invented), and his own sword.

An automaton is a mechanism built to mimic human behavior. They were all the rage in the late 1700s. It is believed the automaton at the Franklin Institute was built by Swiss mechanician Henri Maillardet around 1800. It mysteriously appeared at the institute in November 1928, when a truck delivered the ruins of a complex brass machine to the museum. Donated by the estate of John Penn Brock, the automaton had been in a fire and was in a state of disrepair.

Institute employees painstakingly brought the mechanical boy back to life—and when they did, the automaton began to sketch drawings and write poems. After writing three, two in French, one in English, the automaton signed his work "Ecrit par L'Automate de Maillardet"—"Written by the Automaton of Maillardet."

BIG BEN

WHAT The Franklin Institute, a science museum with an eighteenth-century automaton and the Benjamin Franklin National Memorial

WHERE 222 N. Twentieth St., Philadelphia 19103

COST Museum is adults, $20; children three to eleven, $16. Additional fees for theaters and special exhibits. The rotunda featuring the Benjamin Franklin National Memorial is free.

PRO TIP The Franklin Institute is also home to the second oldest planetarium in North America, for those interested in learning about galaxies far, far away. The museum recently opened the city's largest and most technically advanced games—the Escape Rooms at the Franklin Institute.

26

LITTLE LANDMARKS

Where can you ride Smarty Jones?

Let's start with a little bit of history. Philadelphia was created as a city of squares.

When founder William Penn designed the city, he planned five open-air parks, or squares. They were originally named for their locations—Northwest, Northeast, Southwest, Southeast, and Centre. Although Centre Square, the home of City Hall, kept its name, the others were renamed in 1824 in honor of historic influencers. Thus, we have the current-day designations—Logan, Rittenhouse, Washington, and Franklin squares.

Franklin Square is a great stop for those visiting Philly, especially with children, because it's a playground-like respite in the middle of our historic areas. Junior need to blow off a bit of steam after sitting (somewhat) quietly for the tour of Independence Hall? Reward him with some time at Franklin Square, which is full of kid-sized versions of the city's most important landmarks. The miniature golf course is studded with diminutive versions of Boathouse Row, the Liberty Bell, and the Ben Franklin Bridge.

The hours at Franklin Square are adjusted seasonally, so it's best to check the website when planning a visit. The park also hosts a variety of seasonal activities, including Spooky Mini Golf for Halloween and an Electrical Spectacle Holiday Lights Show for the year-end holidays, beginning in early November.

Make a hole in one at the iconic LOVE Park sculpture, then head over to the Rocky steps at the art museum (in miniature form). ©Scott Lebeau

There are two traditional (and free!) playgrounds on the site, as well, with plenty of benches for the "older folks" to rest their feet while the kids run, jump, and climb. But probably the most fun for Philly fans is the Parx Liberty Carousel, a thirty-animal merry-go-round featuring some of the city's favorites. Besides the traditional horses and patriotically decorated sleighs, you'll see Kentucky Derby winner Smarty Jones and Afleet Alex, winner of the Preakness Stakes and the Belmont Stakes. The most popular ride is on the bald eagle, because Philadelphians are a bit obsessed with their Eagles (and that's no secret!).

27

QUOTH THE RAVEN

What bird contributed to the work of not one but two literary giants?

Creepy black bird? Or messenger from the netherworld?

Who or what, exactly, is Edgar Allan Poe's raven, captured on the page in one of his most famous works, "The Raven?"

We may never know the answer. But we do know where to find the bird that inspired the macabre master. Yes, it's in Philly.

QUOTH THE RAVEN

WHAT Free Library of Philadelphia's Rare Book Department

WHERE 1901 Vine St., Philadelphia 19103

COST Free

PRO TIP Grip can be found on the third floor of the Free Library's Parkway Central Branch. Check out the rare book collection while you're there.

Here's a secret: Before this black bird became Poe's raven, he was an inspiration to another literary master. The raven, named Grip, was the beloved pet of author Charles Dickens and his children. In fact, Dickens enjoyed the bird so much that he included a talking raven in *Barnaby Rudge,* one of his lesser-known works. When Grip died in 1841, Dickens had the bird stuffed and mounted in a window box display.

So where does Poe come

The Free Library of Philadelphia was founded in 1891 and was Philly's first public library system. Today there are fifty-four branches located throughout the city.

A diorama featuring Grip the Raven, pet of author Charles Dickens and inspiration to Edgar Allan Poe, is part of the Rare Book Department at the Free Library of Philadelphia. It was said that Grip had an extensive vocabulary but enjoyed nipping the ankles of the Dickens children. Inset: Dickens apparently enjoyed birds. In addition to the original, he had a second Grip the Raven, as well as an eagle. The tombstone for another bird, Dick, called the "best of birds," is also at the library.
©Max Weidler

in? Well, Edgar reviewed *Barnaby Rudge* and commented that the raven's croaking "might have been prophetically heard through the course of the drama." Poe expanded on that idea and soon after published "The Raven," which sort of put Poe on the map. He did get called out at times for using Dickens's idea, but it didn't seem to matter to those who gathered in fancy salons to hear Poe's dramatic readings of the poem.

So what does all of this have to do with Philadelphia? Well, Poe reviewed *Barnaby Rudge* for a Philly periodical. And today, the shadow box display of Grip the Raven can be seen at the Free Library of Philadelphia in the Rare Book Department, home to collections of both authors' books.

Grip was Poe's inspiration, but Dickens apparently enjoyed birds as pets. The headstone from the grave of Dick, another of Dickens's pet birds, is also on display here.

28

CLOSER TO FREE

Can the creative process bring freedom?

The story is told in four movements on the twenty-foot slab. A figure emerges from the bronze and slowly breaks free, finally standing—joyful, free—away from the wall.

This is *Freedom*, one of the many works of public art Zenos Frudakis has created for the city. The sculpture is a traffic-stopper, striking in both medium and message, and it has been recognized internationally as one of the best pieces of public art.

The sculpture represents a universal human condition: the need to be free, be it from political bondage, an unhealthy situation, or even an internal struggle. And here's a secret: There's an invitation to "get free" extended to all who view the sculpture. The artist left the message to "Stand here" in the cavity left empty by the unbound figure standing free. (It's a great place for photo ops.)

The sculpture is large enough that a passing motorist can catch a glimpse and understand the theme of freedom and escape. But look closer . . . there are more secrets to discover, as the artist made sure there was more going on in his work. "Mini pieces of art" appear throughout

---

Zenos Frudakis's work, including sculptures of Mike Schmidt and Steve Carlton at Citizens Bank Park and the controversial statue of former mayor Frank Rizzo in front of City Hall, can be found throughout the city.

Freedom *encourages all to "break through your mold." It has been called one of the top ten public artworks in the world by the British newspaper* The Independent. *©Scott Lebeau*

CLOSER TO FREE

WHAT *Freedom* sculpture by Zenos Frudakis

WHERE North Sixteenth and Vine streets., Philadelphia 19102

COST Free

PRO TIP The *Freedom* sculpture is in front of a charter school for the performing arts. Vine Street is one way eastbound between Sixteenth and Seventeenth streets.

the wall itself. If you look at the background, you'll find Frudakis's fingerprints all over it. Tools of the sculpture trade can also be found throughout, as well as a variety of heads and figures.

According to his website, Frudakis incorporated work by other artists into the wall. His mother, father, and the cat he had for twenty years also make an appearance.

²⁹ AMERICAN ROYALTY

What princess grew up in Philadelphia?

Before she was the striking actress who turned heads in three Hitchcock classics, before she was the cool blond whose performance in *The Country Girl* won the Academy Award for Best Actress, and long before she married a prince and became a real-life princess, Grace Kelly was already capturing the hearts of her fellow Philadelphians.

Actually, people in the city were smitten with the entire Kelly clan. Patriarch John B. Kelly, called Jack, was a three-time Olympic gold medalist, the first ever in the sport of rowing. Kelly had built a fortune in bricklaying and construction; he and his fashion model-turned-teacher wife, Margaret, raised their four children—Peggy, John (known as Kell), Grace, and LizAnne—in the posh East Falls section of Philadelphia.

They were Philly's own version of the Kennedys, and locals studied their every move. But none more than Grace, who retired from her successful acting career at the age of

AMERICAN ROYALTY

WHAT The childhood home of Princess Grace Kelly

WHERE 3901 Henry Ave., Philadelphia 19129

COST Free

PRO TIP Street parking is readily available in this residential area.

East Falls is also home to three sites listed on the National Register of Historic Places: the Women's Medical College of Pennsylvania, the Thomas Mifflin School, and the historic apartment building Wissahickon.

THE KELLY FAMILY

This famous family lived in the home built here by John B. Kelly. A successful businessman active in city politics, Jack was a 3-time Olympic gold medal winner in the 1920s for rowing. Son John Jr. ("Kell") won the Diamond Scull at the 1947 British Henley Regatta and a bronze medal at the 1956 Olympics. Both father and son were named to US Rowing and Olympic Halls of Fame. Daughter Grace was an Academy Award-winning actress and Princess of Monaco.

PENNSYLVANIA HISTORICAL AND MUSEUM COMMISSION 2011

Grace's mother, Margaret, was the first coach of women's athletic teams at the University of Pennsylvania, but she focused on being a housewife after her marriage. Father Jack Kelly was a Democratic candidate for mayor, but he lost in a tight race. Inset: The marker outside the Kelly family home lists just a few of the occupants' accomplishments. Among others: Grace was the first actress to appear on a US postage stamp.
©Scott Lebeau

twenty-six to marry Prince Rainier III and become the Princess of Monaco. When she died following a stroke and a car accident in 1982, the city mourned one of its own.

A marker stands outside the brick house that the Kelly family used to call home. The six-bedroom house, where Rainier proposed to Grace, has been restored since it fell into disrepair after a subsequent owner, who purchased the house in 1973, was found living in unsanitary conditions in 2013. (She had been living with a colony of cats.)

But—like most fairy tales—it looks like this story may have a happy ending. Reportedly, Prince Albert of Monaco, one of Grace's three children and her only son, purchased the home in 2016, with plans to someday reopen it to the public.

Do you remember the way it used to be?

Pier 18, better known as Graffiti Pier, is the city's largest unsanctioned outdoor art museum. It may also be Philly's worst-kept secret. Formerly used as a place to load coal onto trains during the heyday of the Port Richmond Rail Yards, the pier was abandoned in 1991 by its current owner, Conrail. Yes, this is private property, and anyone on the property is trespassing. And yet they come—the artists who covet wall space for self-expression, the photographers who capture the beauty of that creativity and the nature surrounding it, and, often, the curious, many of whom first appreciate the pier's artwork on social media and come to take selfies.

Philadelphia has seen many eras come and go, from Colonial times through the Gilded Age and up to today's technological society. It's no surprise, then, that some sites are abandoned, left behind as time marches forward. Some rot away, while others are rediscovered, repurposed. Graffiti Pier is poised for resurrection. Long after the train tracks were ripped up, artists have breathed—or spray-painted—fresh life into the area.

Two US presidents were passengers on the SS United States, though at different times. John F. Kennedy and his wife, Jacqueline, traveled on the ship in 1955, prior to his presidency. And a young Bill Clinton was a passenger in 1968, when he went to England to study as a Rhodes Scholar.

Artists tag Graffiti Pier, perhaps the worst-kept secret in the city, with color and creativity. The pier is officially abandoned, though there is interest in making it a public park. Photo courtesy of Kenneth Bell.

Other notable abandoned sites haven't been repurposed—at least, not yet. But they are here, like ghosts in the city, reminding us of days long past, lifestyles now lost to progress. The SS *United States* was, at 650,000 square feet, the largest liner built entirely in the United States. Beginning with her 1952 maiden voyage, the luxury liner enjoyed a celebrated existence, boasting Salvador Dali, Grace Kelly, and Marilyn Monroe among her passengers. But air travel put an end to the popularity of transatlantic ships, and the SS *United States* was docked for good in 1969. The ship was mothballed in 1996 at Philly's Pier 84. Ownership has changed hands numerous times, but plans for the SS *United States* remain uncertain.

LOST BUT NOT FORGOTTEN

WHAT Graffiti Pier, SS *United States*, abandoned sites in Philadelphia

WHERE Separate pier locations on the Delaware River

COST Officially closed to the public

PRO TIP Information about the SS *United States* (which can be viewed legally from across the street) can be found at the website of the SS United States Conservancy, ssusc.org. Numerous people are calling for a repurposing of Graffiti Pier into an official public park. Hidden City Philadelphia (hiddencityphila.org) is a great starting point for learning more.

What summer house played a role in the Revolution–and in a young girl's journal?

Philadelphia wine importer John Wister built the house known as "John Wister's Big House" as a summer residence in 1744, from stone quarried on the property and joists hewn from nearby Wister Woods. Built on fertile soil, the house featured a lush, productive garden and farm that later generations would continue to cultivate.

The patriotic Wister family was not in residence when British general James Agnew commandeered their home and made it his headquarters on the eve of the Battle of Germantown in October 1777. Agnew was fatally shot during General Washington's surprise attack on the British occupiers in Germantown. He was taken back to the Wister house, where he bled out and died in the front parlor. Despite efforts to clean the floorboards, the blood stains remain and are still clearly visible.

One of John's granddaughters, Sarah "Sally" Wister, began keeping a journal when the war interrupted mail service and she could no longer communicate with a friend. Written in letter format, the journal captures the sixteen-year-old's perspective of the Revolution—and of the life of

Outside, visitors can see a massive fruiting ginkgo tree, which towers over the property. Reputed to have grown from a seedling brought from England in 1754, it is known to be one of the oldest in existence in America. Grumblethorpe was named to the National Register of Historic Places in 1972.

Inside "John Wister's Big House," visitors can see period furniture and other treasures belonging to the family. These include a writing desk used by author Owen Wister and a large Victorian dollhouse. Blood stains on the front parlor floor tell of the house's ties to the Revolutionary War. Photo courtesy of PhilaLandmarks.org.

a Quaker teenager in the early days of our country. The journal was published in 1902, almost a hundred years after Sally's death in 1804.

Today, the house is full of treasures belonging to the Wister family, representing their passion for horticulture, science, philanthropy, music, historic preservation, and more. These include a rent receipt from a tenant named Benjamin Franklin, a writing desk used by author Owen Wister, and a giant Victorian dollhouse.

Fun fact: John Wister's grandson, Charles Jones Wister, renamed the property Grumblethorpe after hearing the name in the book *Thinks I to Myself: A Serio-Ludicro, Tragico-Comico Tale*, published in Philadelphia in 1824. Grumblethorpe remains a vibrant center for hands-on education through its elementary education and youth volunteer programs.

DA PLANE! DA PLANE!

Where does a plane crash–and grow?

You can call it irony—the plane, crashed and crumpled, now housing new life.

And you can call it street art—this immense, eye-catching sculpture that appears out of nowhere on a Center City Philly street.

This is Grumman Greenhouse, a decommissioned plane turned greenhouse and the work of Philadelphia's own Jordan Griska, a University of Pennsylvania grad who studied sculpture at the Pennsylvania Academy of the Fine Arts (PAFA). The sculpture is located—or crashed—right outside PAFA, in the open civic space known as Lenfest Plaza.

The Grumman Tracker II was a naval plane designed to bomb submarines during the Cold War era. Built in 1962, the plane measured forty-five feet long, with an impressive seventy-three-foot wingspan. Griska purchased the decommissioned Grumman on eBay and crumpled parts of the front of the plane so it appears to have nosedived into Cherry Street. After changing the form of the Grumman, Griska changed its function, replacing the interior of the cockpit with a working greenhouse. It was installed in 2011.

DA PLANE! DA PLANE!

WHAT Grumman Greenhouse, a sculpture at Lenfest Plaza

WHERE Cherry Street, Philadelphia 19102

COST Free

PRO TIP Tucked away on Cherry Street, it's hard to miss Grumman Greenhouse (believe it or not!). If traveling on Broad, start looking once you spot *Paint Torch* (the giant paintbrush protruding onto Broad Street).

A decommissioned plane-turned-greenhouse, Grumman Greenhouse is a dramatic example of repurposing. ©Max Weidler

The plants in the greenhouse can be seen through the glow of magenta LED lighting, which is powered by solar panels located on the wings. Growing inside are edible vegetables and medicinal herbs provided by the Pennsylvania Horticulture Society.

Bordered by PAFA's Historic Landmark Building and the Samuel P. V. Hamilton Building, Lenfest Plaza is directly across from the Pennsylvania Convention Center. The plaza connects the museums of the Ben Franklin Parkway with the bustling Broad Street crowds.

³³ HOUSE CALL

Where did the Father of American Surgery make his home?

Philadelphia is a city known for its firsts, including many in the medical field. The country's first hospital, Pennsylvania Hospital, opened here in 1751. In 1765, the country's first medical school opened at the University of Pennsylvania.

It comes as no surprise, then, that the man known as the Father of American Surgery made his home in Philly. Philip Syng Physick, born in Philadelphia in 1768, was a 1785 graduate of the University of Pennsylvania. Family legend has it that Dr. Physick wanted to follow in the footsteps of his grandfather, silversmith Philip Syng, maker of the inkwell used to sign the Declaration of Independence. His father, Edmund, had other plans and sent him to England to study with John Hunter, a man who believed anything learned from a textbook could be better learned on a cadaver.

Physick received his medical degree from the University of Edinburgh and, returning to Philadelphia, took a position at Pennsylvania Hospital. Rumors persist that Physick continued his study of cadavers in his own basement, where a room with an entrance to underground tunnels allowed him access to contraband bodies.

The house museum also features a unique collection of early medical tools, some handmade by Dr. Physick. In 1965, with support from Walter and Leonore Annenberg, neighbors, and Physick descendants, the house was restored to the era of Dr. Physick. It is owned and operated by PhilaLandmarks.

Left: The four-story Hill-Physick House is the only freestanding Federal townhouse still standing in Society Hill. Photo courtesy of PhilaLandmarks.

Right: The Philadelphia Society for the Preservation of Landmarks, or PhilaLandmarks, restores, finishes, and presents notable historic house museums to the public. Photo by Mindy Veissid and used courtesy of PhilaLandmarks.

The house was commissioned in 1786 by Henry Hill, executor of Benjamin Franklin's estate. Later, the house was rented to the parents of future Civil War hero George A. McCall, born here in 1802. The house was eventually purchased by Dr. Physick's sister Abigail in 1815. The doctor and his children moved in after he separated from his wife, Elizabeth, and remained until his death in 1837.

Today, visitors come to see the opulent French-influenced Neoclassical furnishings and to hear about the nineteenth-century soap opera that played out in this space. Family history says the doctor forbade his ex-wife from ever entering the house. And was his housekeeper, Annie, really his mistress?

HOUSE CALL

WHAT The Hill-Physick House, a historic house museum

WHERE 321 S. Fourth St., Philadelphia 19106

COST General admission, $8; students and seniors, $6; families, $20

PRO TIP The museum is open Thursday through Sunday, and weekends only in March and December.

ANCHORS AWAY!

Where can you get your sea legs—and learn about maritime history?

When Admiral Dewey fought the Battle of Manila Bay—long considered our country's debut as a world naval power—his flagship was a bit of an orphan.

The protected cruiser *USS Olympia*, originally launched in 1892, had no sister ships, a rare occurrence for naval vessels. Yet the Olympia now stands—or floats—as the sole surviving naval ship of the Spanish-American War.

Also the world's oldest floating steel warship, the *USS Olympia* is now docked at the Independence Seaport Museum, a maritime museum on the Philly side of the Delaware River. The museum, which is dedicated to connecting the community and visitors to the rivers and watersheds of the area, is also home to the submarine *USS Becuna*, which launched in 1943 and completed five wartime patrols. Visitors to the museum are welcome to board these National Historic Landmark ships to experience what

---

Located on the museum's second floor, the J. Welles Henderson Archives and Library allows visitors to learn about maritime history and culture along the Delaware River through personal records, rare books, ship models, and cultural artifacts. Be sure to peruse the Thayer Family Collection, which includes a list of the first-class passengers on the *Titanic* and an April 14, 1932, newspaper clipping titled "Phila. Man Tells of Titanic Wreck."

Hands-on, interactive experiences focusing on water are part of the educational outreach at Independence Seaport Museum. Programs include the Sailor STEM Boatbuilding Program and Floating Wetlands. Photo courtesy Independence Seaport Museum.

ANCHORS AWAY!

WHAT Independence Seaport Museum

WHERE 211 S. Columbus Blvd., Philadelphia 19106

COST Adults, $16; seniors sixty-five and over, $12; children three to twelve, college students, and military, $12; children two and under, free; members, free

PRO TIP Memberships, which start at fifty dollars for an individual and one hundred dollars for a family, also include entrance to the Philadelphia History Museum, making it a shipshape deal.

it was like to navigate life on a warship. (Be warned—living quarters in that submarine were awfully tight!)

Admission to both vessels is included when you visit the museum, where you can learn the history of the port, from the noble (it was a gateway entrance for immigrants in previous years) to the sad (the same port was a large entry point for slaves). Interactive experiences allow visitors to learn to navigate ships through the river. A working boat shop lets you watch the experts as they build and repair vessels, while you can learn about the ecosystem of the Delaware River in the Citizen Science Lab.

But the historic vessels are the highlight of the visit—and a reminder of what life was like for those serving our country.

35 PICTURE YOURSELF IN PHILLY

Where can you take a selfie with some of the city "icons"?

PICTURE YOURSELF IN PHILLY

WHAT Iconic Philadelphia photo ops at the Independence Visitor Center

WHERE 599 Market St. (the corner of Sixth and Market streets, in Independence National Historical Park), Philadelphia 19106

COST Free

PRO TIP Free films at the Visitor Center allow you to sit back and relax, making this a great place to beat the heat if you're visiting in the summer. There's also a café on site if you're getting hungry and a gift store stocked with official Philly souvenirs (if your pictures aren't enough).

Say "Cheese!" (Or, more appropriately, say, "Cheesesteak!")

Managed by the National Park Service, the Independence Visitor Center is a hub of information for those who are visiting Philly. Sure, you can expect brochures, kiosks, and films informing you of all that's going on in the City of Brotherly Love. But did you know that the center is also a great place to take a selfie with several of Philly's iconic characters?

Inside the center, you'll find replicas of some of Philly's finest, including a serious-looking Ben Franklin, a triumphant Rocky Balboa, and the Phillie Phanatic, perhaps the most recognizable team mascot in sports. And if you're ready for this year's holiday photos, a large postcard with "Greetings from Philadelphia" inscribed on it is available as a backdrop, with X's and O's (or "kisses and hugs") you can pose behind.

Yes, it's cheesy (as in "wit whiz"), but it's also a lot of fun, and the pics make great souvenirs. Kids love the caricature-

Wishing you were here . . . make your own postcard using the selfie-worthy photo ops found at the Independence Visitor Center. ©Mary Dixon Lebeau

like statues, and it's a good place to take a break while you're visiting the historic area.

Of course, the Independence Visitor Center is a valuable resource for anyone visiting the city. Steps away from the Liberty Bell, the National Constitution Center, and other historic sites, the center is the only place where you can get free timed-entry tickets to Independence Hall, which are required for entry from March through December.

It's no secret—the Independence Visitor Center is the best first stop when you're visiting Philly, and not just for the photo ops! Here's where you'll pick up your maps, peruse brochures, buy attraction tickets, book tours, make hotel reservations, or discuss your plans with informed visitor services representatives.

WHEN IRISH EYES ARE CRYING

Where is heartbreak and hope captured in a single sculpture?

It was called *An Gorta Mór*—the Great Hunger. When the potato crop failed in Ireland in 1845, it brought on a period of great famine in the country, the beginning of seven years of starvation. During this dark, sad period, more than a million people died in Ireland, and another million fled the country.

The hopelessness, the heartbreak, and the hunger of that period are captured in Glenna Goodacre's sculpture, the Irish Memorial, which graces a corner at Front and Chestnut streets. The piece is an impressive thirty feet long, with thirty-five characters in bronze telling the story of the suffering of the Irish during the famine and their subsequent arrival on the shores of our country.

As you venture around the sculpture's base, you will see the story played out in front of you—first, the haunting, anguished looks on the faces of those still in Ireland, some digging in the ground scrounging for food, others desperately pleading as the potatoes continue to be exported to other countries, many already dead and buried

Artist Glenna Goodacre also designed the Vietnam Women's Memorial, located a short walk from the Reflecting Pool in Washington, DC. The Irish Memorial was constructed to commemorate the sesquicentennial of the Great Hunger.

The Irish Memorial tells a story in its flow; you travel from hunger to hope as you walk around the thirty-foot monument. ©Scott Lebeau

beneath Celtic crosses. Continue around to see the ship full of anxious, hopeful Irish as they embark on a journey to America and finally rush forward, hungry for the opportunity to escape their suffering.

The sculpture was unveiled on October 25, 2003, and is dedicated to the memory of those who perished in Ireland as well as those who made it to our country's shore. It is also a nod to Philly's large Irish population.

WHEN IRISH EYES ARE CRYING

WHAT The Irish Memorial

WHERE South Front and Chestnut streets., Philadelphia 19106

COST Free

PRO TIP The Irish Memorial shares a small park with the National Scottish Immigrants' Memorial, which commemorates the contributions of Scottish immigrants to American society. Both sculptures are within walking distance of many well-known tourist attractions, including the Betsy Ross House and Independence Hall.

37 BUTCHERS, BAKERS, BARGAINS, AND BALBOA

Where can you visit one of the oldest open-air markets in the country?

Two words come to mind when you visit the Italian Market in South Philly. The first is "authentic"—no tourist trap here. And the second is "fresh."

The freshest meats, cheeses, baked goods, candies, produce, and pasta are the wares of the vendors lining Ninth Street for about ten blocks. Exploring these blocks is like taking a culinary journey through the freshest foods Philly has to offer. The fish is freshly caught, the eggs arrive fresh from the farm, and the crusty bread is fresh from the oven. Dozens of merchants line the streets, selling everything from high-quality meats to homemade mozzarella and from handcrafted chocolates to cannoli and gelato.

The Italian Market launched in the 1880s to serve the growing population of Italian immigrants settling in South Philly. Shops opened to provide the new residents with the food staples they were accustomed to—fresh cheeses,

---

Don't be fooled by the "Italian" title. Though the market originally opened to serve Italian immigrants in South Philly, it has become quite diverse through the years. Alongside the pasta and gelato, you'll now find such tasty treats as Vietnamese pho, authentic Mexican fare, and Korean barbecue.

BUTCHERS, BAKERS, BARGAINS, AND BALBOA

WHAT The Italian Market, an authentic street market featured in several *Rocky* movies

WHERE Ninth Street between Wharton and Fitzwater

COST Free to roam, and plenty of bargains to be found!

PRO TIP The market is open seven days a week, year-round, though some vendors close on Mondays.

cured meats, produce, olive oil, and other Italian favorites. Even today, the butcher shops feature the carcasses of newly slaughtered pigs and cows, a testament to the freshness and authenticity of the food.

Though its Italian roots are still quite prominent, the market today is more than just a street corner grocery mart. Several restaurants are located in the market or nearby, allowing busy shoppers to satisfy any hunger they build up perusing the streets for a bargain. There's something for every appetite, from French and Italian to Mexican and Middle Eastern—along with the standard pizza and (of course) cheesesteaks.

Rocky fans will remember the Italian Market from several of the movies in the series. The Italian Stallion jogged through the shops on Ninth Street as part of his training and famously practiced his punch on a side of beef at one of the butcher shops here.

GOLDEN GLOVES

Who's the other boxer honored with a statue in Philly?

Before Rocky Balboa ever appeared on the silver screen, Joe Frazier was smoking up the boxing rings in Philadelphia. And, unlike Sylvester Stallone's celluloid hero, Joe Frazier was real!

Smokin' Joe Frazier, as he was known, was actually born in Beaufort, South Carolina, on January 12, 1944. As a teenager, he moved by himself to Philadelphia. It was here that he began his amateur boxing career, winning the Golden Gloves Heavyweight Championships in 1962, 1963, and 1964. In '64, he went to the Summer Olympics in Tokyo as an alternate; he ended up replacing heavyweight Buster Mathis, who was injured. Frazier won the only boxing gold medal the United States took home that year—and, unbeknownst to most, he fought the final match with a broken left thumb.

Joe was the undisputed heavyweight champion from 1970 to 1973, but he may be best remembered for his series of three matches against fellow heavyweight Muhammed Ali in the early and mid-'70s. The first, touted as "The Fight

---

In 1967, Frazier took part in the first sporting event held at the late great Philly Spectrum. His gym, where Frazier trained for many of his fights, still stands at 2917 North Broad Street and is on the National Register of Historic Places. Although the building has housed a furniture store in recent years, Frazier fans can still glimpse the champ's name on the side of the building.

The twelve-foot-tall, eighteen-hundred-pound bronze statue of Joe Frazier is the work of Philly artist Stephen Layne. ©Scott Lebeau

of the Century," took place on March 8, 1971, at Madison Square Garden in New York, with Frazier coming out victorious in a unanimous decision. The second, in January 1974, was a non-titled fight, which Ali won. Their final meeting in the ring was the much-publicized "Thrilla in Manila," held on October 1, 1975, in the Philippines. Ali was declared the winner in a TKO (technical knockout) before the fifteenth round.

Frazier retired in 1981 but continued as a boxing trainer and mentor in Philadelphia. He ran a gym in the city that produced numerous notable fighters, including heavyweight champion Michael Spinks. Frazier lost his final fight—this time with liver cancer—on November 7, 2011.

The statue, which depicts Joe Frazier as he looked when he defeated Ali in their first meeting, was unveiled on September 12, 2015. Many fans thought the tribute was long overdue. After all, why was the city so quick to honor a fictional boxer—and so slow when it came to paying tribute to the real deal?

GOLDEN GLOVES

WHAT Statue of Joe Frazier, iconic heavyweight boxer

WHERE Outside XFINITY Live!, 1100 Pattison Ave., Philadelphia 19148

COST Free

PRO TIP XFINITY Live! is a premier dining establishment in the heart of the South Philly stadiums, where the Eagles, Phillies, Flyers, and 76ers play. If you're just going to get a selfie with Smokin' Joe, check the sports calendars to avoid stadium traffic.

39

FLY, EAGLES, FLY

Is there room for an animal habitat in this city of neighborhoods?

Philadelphia is a city obsessed with its eagles—and not just those fighting it out on the NFL gridiron.

Close to the Philadelphia International Airport, a pair of mated bald eagles can be spotted soaring. These are just two of the numerous birds, amphibians, mammals, reptiles, and fish that have found a home at John Heinz National Wildlife Refuge, a thousand acres of woods, wetlands, marshes, and meadows dedicated to wildlife protection. More than eighty species of birds, including egrets, sandpipers, and, yes, eagles, have made nests there, and the diverse habitats also provide refuge for a variety of wildlife, from deer and mink to the southern leopard frog and the rare red-bellied turtle.

For humans, too, the wildlife refuge provides a breath of fresh air on the edge of the hectic city. Anglers fish for catfish and carp in Darby Creek. (You can borrow a fishing pole for free from the Visitor Center.) A canoe ramp allows easy access to the waters for canoers and kayakers, while

---

The Cusano Environmental Education Center provides environmental education to local children. It is named for Philly resident Anthony Cusano, who left his entire estate to the Department of the Interior for this purpose. The refuge itself was renamed in 1991 in honor of Senator John Heinz, a champion of the Tinicum Marsh.

FLY, EAGLES, FLY

WHAT John Heinz National Wildlife Refuge at Tinicum

WHERE 8601 Lindbergh Blvd., Philadelphia 19153

COST Free

PRO TIP The refuge is open from sunrise to sunset daily.

Dioramas in the Visitor Center feature some of the area's inhabitants.
©Mary Dixon Lebeau

runners and joggers pace themselves on ten miles of trails through the refuge.

The Lenape Indians first lived on this land, which once consisted of nearly six thousand acres of marshland. In the early seventeenth century, European farmers who settled here drained the marshes and filled them in to provide land for grazing. By the 1960s, the construction of I-95 threatened the remaining marshland—only two hundred acres!—and environmentally conscious citizens fought to save it. With the help of some members of Congress, they succeeded in getting the highway rerouted. The area was named a National Natural Landmark in 1965 and opened as a wildlife preserve called the Tinicum National Environmental Center in 1972.

Today, the renamed John Heinz National Wildlife Refuge at Tinicum provides refuge for many species—including the people who can visit and be renewed in the great outdoors.

40

HELLO, HELLO, HELLO . . . HELLO

Which of the Stooges was born on South Street?

"Ooooh, a wise guy, eh?"

Well, they may not have been wise, but the Three Stooges certainly were funny . . . especially to those who enjoyed the rowdy, somewhat violent vaudeville humor that the trio brought to life. There were actually six men, or stooges, featured in the act's almost fifty-year run (from 1922 to 1970), but for most people, there were only three who really counted—Larry, Moe, and Curly.

Moe and Curly were the Howard brothers, while Larry was Philadelphia's own Larry Fine. Fine was born Louis Feinberg on October 5, 1902, right at Third and South streets. The building now houses Jon's Bar & Grille, but there's a mural of the crazy-haired Stooge playing his violin outside the establishment—a must-see for all Stooge fans.

Larry gained a lot of attention with his violin, winning local amateur nights and eventually performing as a violinist in vaudeville. It was there that he met his first Howard—

As a child, Larry, the son of a jeweler, severely burned his forearm with acid that his father used to test the purity of gold. The Feinbergs had their son take violin lessons to strengthen his damaged muscles. So when you see the Three Stooges playing fiddle in one of their approximately two hundred short films, only two are faking. Fine was an accomplished musician.

Fuzzy-haired Stooge Larry Fine was actually a fine musician, having taken violin lessons to build strength in a burnt arm. He took up boxing for the same reason. ©Mary Dixon Lebeau

Shemp, Moe's brother, who was performing at the time with Ted Healy's Stooges in the revue *A Night in Venice*. Howard was leaving and needed a replacement; Fine took the gig, and history was born. He and Moe became the anchors of the group, with others taking the role of the third Stooge as needed.

Fine, with his bald dome surrounded by bushy red curls, is one of the more recognizable Stooges. His Stooge character was often the voice of reason when Moe's bullying or Curly's whimpering got out of hand. Fine suffered a stroke in January 1970 that left him paralyzed on the left side and ended his entertainment career. He died five years later at a nursing home in Woodland Hills and is buried in the Forest Lawn Memorial Park.

But Fine's memory lives on in the Stooge shorts, and he is immortalized in the mural above his birthplace. Another tip of the hat to Fine—he was named to Central High School's Hall of Fame in October 2009—even though he never completed high school.

HELLO, HELLO, HELLO . . . HELLO

WHAT The Larry Fine birthplace and mural

WHERE Jon's Bar & Grille, 300 South St., Philadelphia 19147

COST Free

PRO TIP Larry Fine wasn't Philadelphia's only representative in the Stooges. Joe DeRita, who went by the name Curly-Joe, was the final Stooge, working with Larry and Moe from 1958 to 1970. DeRita is a Philly guy, too—though there's no mural for Curly-Joe (yet!).

41

TEARS IN HEAVEN

Where can you find the saddest spot in the city?

Many may argue that the saddest place in Philly is Lincoln Financial Field, home of the Eagles, after any loss to the Cowboys. But we don't expect that to happen too often.

TEARS IN HEAVEN

WHAT Laurel Hill Cemetery

WHERE 3822 Ridge Ave., Philadelphia 19132

COST Free (but a $5 guide is available and helpful!)

PRO TIP Families with children should stop by the office to pick up a free activity pack or download the I-Spy Tombstone Hunt worksheet online.

The true saddest spot in the city is on a hill overlooking the murky waters of the Schuylkill River. There, a tribute sculpture depicts a mother holding her infant twins. The memorial, carved by the woman's husband and the twins' father, is positioned so that the mother is gazing out at the dark waters—at the very spot where the babies drowned. As in life, Mary Schaaff remains in death, forever searching for her lost children.

This remarkable monument is just one of the beautiful death-as-art tributes found at Laurel Hill Cemetery. The cemetery, a gorgeous park

Laurel Hill Cemetery spreads out for ninety-five acres overlooking the Schuylkill. Every tombstone tells a story, and the sad, beautiful architecture of Laurel Hill echoes the stories of Philadelphia's history. From the notable to the nobody, each rests in peace surrounded by haunting memorials and beautiful horticulture.

Harry Kalas first joined the Phillies organization in 1971. He was master of ceremonies at the opening of Veterans Stadium on April 10, 1971. He threw out the opening pitch of a game on April 8, 2009, and died five days later. ©Mary Dixon Lebeau Inset: There are inscriptions in Polish and English on the Mother and Twins monument. Many are too worn to read. One that can be made out says, "We should count time in heart throbs. He most lives who thinks most." ©Scott Lebeau

full of history, horticulture, and remarkable architecture, was founded because of a similar sadness. One of the founders, librarian John Jay Smith, complained of Philadelphia graveyards in 1835, noting that he couldn't identify the resting place of his own daughter in the overcrowded Friends graveyard on Cherry Street. Less than a year later, this grieving father and three partners founded Laurel Hill Cemetery as a spacious and peaceful alternative to the crowded churchyards where most people were buried at the time.

The cemetery is now the final home of historical figures such as General George Meade and thirty-nine other Civil War generals, as well as to six *Titanic* passengers and at least one Philly pop cultural icon—Harry Kalas, Hall of Fame broadcaster and voice of the Phillies for thirty-eight years, whose grave is marked with a giant microphone and two seats from Veterans Stadium (also departed).

42

PIPE DREAMS

Where can you hear pipe organ music played mightily– while you shop?

Twice a day, lucky shoppers at Macy's in Center City Philadelphia are treated to a flourish of pipe organ music while they consider the latest fashions or try on a pair of shoes.

That's because Macy's is home to the Wanamaker Grand Court Organ, one of the world's largest fully functioning pipe organs. Originally built for the 1904 St. Louis World's Fair, the organ was purchased in 1909 by city merchant John Wanamaker, founder of the now-defunct Wanamaker's department store. He hired a crew to make the organ even bigger, working in a private organ factory installed in the store's attic. The organ now stands over the grand court of the historic seven-story department building, which has changed hands a couple of times and is now Macy's Center City.

During the holiday season, the pipe organ shares the spotlight as Macy's celebrates the holiday season with its Christmas Light Show and Wanamaker Organ Concert, an area family holiday tradition for more than fifty years. Along with the wonderful organ music, visitors delight in the stories-high images of snowflakes, a toy shop, ballerinas, and Santa Claus, accompanied by a soundtrack featuring Julie Andrews.

Macy's Center City is home to the Wanamaker Grand Court Organ, which was purchased by Philadelphia merchant John Wanamaker in 1909. Photo by Olivia Brosky and used courtesy of Macy's Inc.

The building itself, still known as the Wanamaker Building, is a throwback to the days when shopping was a true event. Wanamaker's was the city's first department store and one of the first in the country, opening its doors in 1911. President William Taft officially dedicated the store on December 30 of that year, and city shoppers clamored for the glamour of the store's nine retail floors (with an additional three for office space). The building was designated a National Historic Landmark in 1978.

The store today has a lot less retail space—just the first three floors. But you can still find a footstone commemorating the 1911 dedication. And, of course, you can still hear the organ play, its grand music floating over the shoppers just as it did a century ago.

PIPE DREAMS

WHAT Wanamaker Grand Court Organ at Macy's Center City

WHERE Macy's, 1300 Market St., Philadelphia 19107

COST Free

PRO TIP Listen to the music while snapping pictures at the beloved Wanamaker Eagle, a 2,500-pound bronze statue of an eagle (a bird, not a football player) that has long been a favorite meeting place for shoppers: "Let's meet in twenty at the Eagle." It's currently located in the Macy's shoe department.

43 CARUSO REDIVIVUS!

What ever happened to the city's favorite tenor?

Philly has major ties with the music industry, but when many people think of TSOP (that's "the sound of Philadelphia"), they think of rock and roll. After all, the city was the home of Chubby Checker, the American half of the original Live Aid concert, and the institution known as *American Bandstand,* just to name a few.

But our music roots are much deeper. Popular music came out of the city way before the birth of rock and roll. And one of the area's earliest music stars was Philly-born tenor Mario Lanza. Born Alfredo Arnold Cocozza on January 31, 1921, Lanza rose to fame in the forties and fifties as a singer and movie star.

Classically trained at an early age, Lanza began appearing in operatic productions at a Philly YMCA in his teens. He was discovered in 1942 by visiting conductor Serge Koussevitzky who, upon hearing the tenor, murmured, "Caruso redivivus!" ("Caruso reborn!"). Young Freddy changed his name to Mario Lanza, the masculine form of Maria Lanza, his

---

The museum is just the first stop for Mario Lanza fans. A mural at the corner of Broad and Reed depicts pinnacle moments in Lanza's life and career. A marker stands outside his birthplace on Christian Street. And Mario Lanza Park (formerly Queen Street Park) is located on Queen Street between Second and Third—a short walk from the singer's birthplace.

Mario Lanza began his musical career in Philadelphia and was a member of the inaugural class of the Music Alliance Walk of Fame. Photo courtesy of the Mario Lanza Institute and Museum.

mother's maiden name, and a star was born.

But not so fast . . . the budding singer was drafted and served in World War II, performing in Army productions and resuming his career upon his release. He performed as the tenor in an operatic trio until 1947, when Louis B. Mayer offered Lanza a seven-year movie deal. He made eight films with MGM before his untimely death following a heart attack in 1959 at the age of thirty-eight.

CARUSO REDIVIVUS!

WHAT The Mario Lanza Institute and Museum

WHERE 712 Montrose St., Philadelphia

COST $5 a person

PRO TIP The museum is only open on select dates or by appointment. Check the website for dates or call 215-238-9691 for an appointment.

Lanza's career was short, but it left its mark, both on the world of opera and on his hometown. The Mario Lanza Institute and Museum celebrates the singer's life with a collection of memorabilia, including lobby cards, costumes, and a terra-cotta bust.

HANDS-ON HISTORY

Is there a historic building where kids are encouraged to touch everything?

Today, kids have taken over Memorial Hall. They push carts through their own mini-supermarket, head through a rabbit hole to join the Mad Hatter for tea, and ride trolleys by kid-centric roadside attractions. They learn a lot, they have a blast—and they may be oblivious to the history that surrounds them as they play.

Since October 2008, the Please Touch Museum has made its home in West Fairmount Park in historic Memorial Hall. The hall was originally built as an art gallery for the 1876 Centennial Exposition, the country's first time hosting a world's fair. President Ulysses S. Grant was on hand at the opening ceremonies in May 1876. Of the many exhibition halls created for the 1876 Centennial Exposition, only Memorial Hall remains.

Closing after the Expo, Memorial Hall reopened in 1877, serving as home to both the Philadelphia Museum School of Industrial Art and the Philadelphia Museum of Art (which moved in 1929). Through the years, the building has served a variety of purposes, including a gymnasium, a basketball court, a recording hall for the Philadelphia Orchestra, and a police station. It was even the site of the 1997 viewing of

The Statue of Liberty's torch was displayed under the dome at Memorial Hall during the 1876 Centennial Exposition. Today, a replica of the torch—made completely of toys—occupies the same space.

Memorial Hall was designed by Hermann J. Schwarzmann, chief engineer of Fairmount Park at the time. It is made of glass, iron, brick, and granite. ©Scott Lebeau

former Phillies player-turned-long-time-announcer Richie Ashburn.

The Please Touch Museum renovated the hall and moved here from its previous location on Twenty-First Street. And it looks like the kids are here to stay, breathing life into this old granite and marble hall. In 2005, the Please Touch Museum signed an eighty-year lease with the city, guaranteeing that arts and crafts will continue in this old art gallery for decades to come.

HANDS-ON HISTORY

WHAT Memorial Hall and the Please Touch Museum, a historic landmark now housing a hands-on children's museum

WHERE 4231 Avenue of the Republic, Philadelphia 19131

COST Adults and children one and older, $19; members and children under one, free; carousel rides, $3 per ride or unlimited rides for $5

PRO TIP The Please Touch Museum offers a variety of ways to save money on admission. Check its website for current offers. If you visit on the first Wednesday of the month during its extended hours (4 p.m. to 7 p.m.), admission is only two dollars per person!

BIG BEN *The dramatic statue of Benjamin Franklin in the rotunda of the Franklin Institute weighs thirty tons and sits on a ninety-two-ton marble pedestal.* ©*Scott Lebeau*

WHERE THE KOI ARE *Visitors tour the house (no shoes, please!), visit the tea house, and feed the koi in the pond outside Shofuso. Tea ceremony demonstrations give insight into this ancient ritual.* ©Scott Lebeau

CASTLES ON A CLOUD *Many cigar store figurines are part of Henry Mercer's collection. In the second half of the nineteenth century, these were used to advertise the wares of the stores they stood outside. Photo courtesy of the Mercer Museum and Library.*

PICTURE YOURSELF IN PHILLY *Even in the off-season, Phillies mascot the Phillie Phanatic (or a replica) can be found at Independence Visitor Center, so have your cameras ready.*
©Mary Dixon Lebeau

EVERYDAY HEROES *A visit to the National Liberty Museum includes a glimpse into the secret hiding place shared by Anne Frank and her family.* ©Mary Dixon Lebeau

LIGHTS, CAMERA, PHILLY Clothespin, *a sculpture by Claes Oldenburg, can be spotted in the Eddie Murphy/Dan Ackroyd movie* Trading Places. ©*Scott Lebeau*

WHERE PILGRIMS PRAY *Stained-glass windows in the National Shrine of St. John Neumann illustrate the story of his life, including his first mass, missionary work, and ordination as a bishop.* ©Scott Lebeau

OH, DEM GOLDEN SLIPPERS *Mummers' costumes are elaborate and detailed, often made of satin and including elements of Mylar and metal. Sequins and feathers are favorite finishing touches.* ©Mary Dixon Lebeau

THE BIGGER, THE BETTER *A dollop of paint on the pavement seems to have dripped from Paint Torch, a Claes Oldenburg sculpture.* ©Max Weidler

THIS LITTLE PIGGY WENT TO MARKET *Philbert the Pig gobbles up coins for local charities in the middle of the seating area at Reading Terminal Market. Here, you can feast on everything from pulled pork sandwiches and tiramisu cupcakes to gourmet grilled-cheese sandwiches and fluffernutter whoopie pies. ©Mary Dixon Lebeau*

OUR CITY, OUR TEAMS *The skill of the team, the support of the city, and the enthusiasm of the fans—all are captured in the sports murals that grace various walls in Philadelphia.*
©Mary Dixon Lebeau

GIANT FOOD *Iconic South Street store Zipperhead is long gone, but its creepy ants still crawl the building.* ©Scott Lebeau

TOOTHY GRINS *This bucket of teeth reportedly was at Edgar R. R. Parker's feet when he lectured during his "Parker Dental Show."* ©Scott Lebeau

· E V A N S ·

IN MEMORY OF
DR. THOMAS WILLIAM EVANS
FOUNDER OF
THE THOMAS W. EVANS MUSEUM AND DENTAL INSTITUTE
AND OF AGNES DOYLE EVANS HIS WIFE
IN THE VAULT AT THE FOOT OF THIS MONUMENT LIE THE BODIES OF

DR. THOMAS W. EVANS 1823–1897	MAJOR WM. M. EVANS 1792–1882
AND HIS WIFE	CATHARINE A. EVANS 1792–1878
AGNES DOYLE EVANS 1822–1897	MRS. ANNIE O'CONNOR DIED – 1892

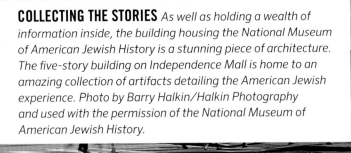

COLLECTING THE STORIES *As well as holding a wealth of information inside, the building housing the National Museum of American Jewish History is a stunning piece of architecture. The five-story building on Independence Mall is home to an amazing collection of artifacts detailing the American Jewish experience. Photo by Barry Halkin/Halkin Photography and used with the permission of the National Museum of American Jewish History.*

WHEN IRISH EYES ARE CRYING *A plaque nearby quotes poet Peter Quinn's "Remembrance," which concludes, "We have it in our power, not only to remember what took place but to relive it . . . To find in the hungry and lost, not a different race . . . But the faces of our ancestors . . . an image of ourselves." ©Scott Lebeau*

What is the Mercer Mile?

When creating the design for our new country, the Founding Fathers charted a new course from what they knew, forgoing a monarchy for a democracy. It might seem a bit ironic, then, that right outside Philadelphia there is a wonderful castle.

Fonthill Castle is not the home of royalty, of course. Instead, it was the home of Henry Chapman Mercer, who called it a "Castle for a New World." It is a showplace for Mercer's collection of tiles and prints. The house itself, built between 1908 and 1912, is on the National Register of Historic Places and is one of the earliest examples of poured-in-place concrete.

The castle, which boasts forty-four rooms, eighteen fireplaces, and more than two hundred windows, can only be seen during a guided tour. Although much of the house's original pastel paint has fallen victim to the years, one room has been restored so visitors can view it as Mercer did. The archeologist's extensive collection of ceramics and artifacts can be seen on and in the house.

Mercer Mile goes beyond the tilemaker's castle-home. The Mercer Museum, a six-story fortress of poured-in-place

---

The Mercer Mile actually consists of three historical attractions—the Fonthill Castle, the Mercer Museum, and the Moravian Pottery and Tile Works, a working museum where tiles are still made. Tours are available every half hour.

Fonthill Castle is a unique professional museum and National Historic Landmark that attracts more than thirty thousand visitors each year. Photo by Nic Barlow.

concrete, houses more than forty thousand early American artifacts, from whaling boats to a Conestoga wagon. Favorites among the extensive collection include the displays on animal husbandry, fishing and trapping, blacksmithing, and a general store.

CASTLES ON A CLOUD

WHAT The Mercer Mile, including Fonthill Castle and Mercer Museum

WHERE Castle, 525 E. Court St., Doylestown 18901; museum, 84 S. Pine St., Doylestown 18901

COST Fonthill Castle—adults, $15; seniors (sixty-five and up), $13; youth (six to seventeen), $8; five and under, free. Hour-long guided tours. Call 215-348-9461 for reservations. Mercer Museum—adults, $15; seniors (sixty-five and up), $13; youth (six to seventten), $8; five and under, free.

PRO TIP A Mercer Experience Ticket, including admission to both attractions, is available. Adults, $26; youth, $15.

ONLY GOD CAN MAKE A TREE

How does your garden grow?

The word arboretum means "a botanical garden devoted to trees." However, that term has been redefined in the ninety-two lavish acres spanning a historic landscape on the edge of Philadelphia's Chestnut Hill neighborhood. Originally known as Compton and built in 1887, the private estate was the summer home of John and Lydia T. Morris, siblings who created the sumptuously landscaped environment using plants and techniques they learned in their international travels. The estate became a public arboretum in 1932, when it was acquired by the University of Pennsylvania.

Today, more than twelve thousand living plants thrive on the property, including some that can be traced back to those that John Morris planted. Visitors leave the urban hustle behind when they visit this plush oasis in the middle of the concrete forest. Deeply breathe the sweet scent of the American beauties in the well-tended rose garden. If you're quiet—and lucky!—a pair of swans may glide by while you meditate near the tranquil swan pond. Wetlands and meadows provide a great

The Dorrance H. Hamilton Fernery is the only remaining freestanding Victorian fernery in North America. Photo by Paul Meyer, courtesy Morris Arboretum of the University of Pennsylvania.

habitat for birds, so bring your binoculars to spot such visitors as Baltimore orioles, Carolina chickadees, and Canada geese.

Another favorite is the Morris Arboretum's Tree Adventure Exhibit, a birds-eye view of life in the upper canopy of the trees. Kids of all ages climb the treetops (netting makes this safe) and enjoy checking out the human-sized bird's nest complete with huge bright blue eggs.

A variety of self-guided tours and interactive family experiences are available, both at the Widener Visitor Center and on the website. Don't miss the Dorrance H. Hamilton Fernery, the only freestanding Victorian fernery remaining in North America. Designed and built in 1899, the fernery reflects the Victorian-era obsession with glasshouses and ferns.

UPON THIS ROCK

Who was Richard Allen, and how did he bring worshippers out of the balcony?

The founder of Mother Bethel African Methodist Episcopal Church, Richard Allen, was born a slave on Valentine's Day in 1760 in Philadelphia, the son of a biracial mother and an African father.

At the age of seventeen, Allen, who was permitted to attend church services, became a Christian and joined the Methodist Society. Freed from the wages of sin—though still a slave—Allen and his brother worked even harder on the plantation to disprove the myth that Christian slaves were useless. Because of this, Allen's owner allowed Allen to invite Methodist preachers to hold worship services in his home. The owner eventually converted to Christianity as well and allowed the Allen brothers to buy their freedom.

Once freed, Allen became a preacher, drawing many black congregants to St. George's Methodist Episcopal Church in Philadelphia. White church elders decided to ease the overcrowding via segregation, building a new balcony for the black worshippers to use, sometimes even interrupting their prayers to direct them to the upper seats. Instead, the black congregants formed their own church, with the backing of notable colonists including Benjamin Rush, Robert Ralston, and, eventually, George Washington.

Through the years, the church has hosted a variety of notable speakers, from Frederick Douglass to Rev. Martin Luther King Jr. The church was designated a National Historic Landmark in 1974.

MOTHER BETHEL AFRICAN METHODIST EPISCOPAL CHURCH

According to the church's Facebook page, the mission of the African Methodist Episcopal Church is to minister to the spiritual, intellectual, physical, emotional, and environmental needs of all people through spreading Christ's liberating gospel through word and deed. ©Scott Lebeau

UPON THIS ROCK

WHAT Mother Bethel African Methodist Episcopal Church, home of the country's first black denomination and the oldest parcel of land in the United States continuously owned by African Americans

WHERE 419 S. Sixth St., Philadelphia 19147

COST Free (donations encouraged)

PRO TIP Mother Bethel AME Church holds worship every Sunday morning at 9:30 a.m. Church school begins before the service, at 8. Sunday School is available for children during the service.

Mother Bethel AME Church, founded in 1787, was the nation's first independent Protestant denomination founded by African Americans. Through the years, the church has been active in the Civil Rights movement, from offering refuge to escaped Jamaican slaves in 1795 to providing support to the Underground Railroad.

Today, the church also houses the Richard Allen Museum, which includes the basement crypt that contains Allen's tomb, as well as that of his wife, Sarah. Other artifacts in the museum include Allen's original pulpit, old ballot boxes used in church elections, and pews from the early days of the church. Members of the current congregation volunteer to give tours and tell Allen's story.

48 LIGHTS, CAMERA, PHILLY

Where have you seen this place before?

Call it the *Rocky* effect. After all, everyone remembers that run through the Italian Market, down the streets of South Philly, and up the steps of the Philadelphia Museum of Art.

But the city wasn't a newcomer to film when *Rocky* took the Best Picture Oscar in 1976. Even before Katharine Hepburn, Jimmy Stewart, and Cary Grant showed off the Main Line in 1940's *The Philadelphia Story*, Philadelphia had been a popular locale for filmmakers.

Want to check out the locations that appear in some of your favorite films? Here's where to start.

Begin with the movie that shares the city's name. *Philadelphia* was the 1993 Jonathan Demme drama starring Oscar-winner Tom Hanks, Denzel Washington, and our fair city. From the opening montage, featuring the Ben Franklin Bridge, Liberty Place, and the Liberty Bell, to the Pickwick Pharmacy and Mt. Sinai Hospital, to the film's climactic courthouse scene filmed in City Hall, Philadelphia steals scene after scene.

An earlier drama, 1981's *Blow Out*, featured John Travolta, John Lithgow, and a host of Philly sites. Look for the Wissahickon Bridge, City Hall, the Independence Seaport

---

Homeboy M. Night Shyamalan has shot all his films in the Philadelphia area, including *Unbreakable* ('00), *The Village* ('04), *After Earth* ('13), and *Split* ('16). On the lighter side, *Transformers 2: Revenge of the Fallen* includes scenes shot at the University of Pennsylvania, Laurel Hill Cemetery, and the Italian Market.

Philadelphia's City Hall has been featured in numerous popular movies, including Philadelphia *and* Blow Out. *©Scott Lebeau*

LIGHTS, CAMERA, PHILLY

WHAT Movie sites

WHERE A variety of places throughout the city

COST Free

PRO TIP A cottage industry has sprung up throughout the city, offering tours of movie locations (especially *Rocky*, of course). These can be found on the internet for those who don't want to put together their own tour.

Museum, and Macy's. Two years later, the Dan Ackroyd/Eddie Murphy comedy *Trading Places* featured the Schuylkill Expressway and Boathouse Row in its opening. Other Philly sites in the movie include the Old Fidelity Bank and *Clothespin*, a sculpture outside City Hall—and who can forget the scenes of Eddie Murphy begging in Rittenhouse Square?

National Treasure (2004) put a spotlight on Philly's historical area, featuring Independence Hall, Reading Terminal Market, Old Pine Street Church, and the Franklin Institute. Haley Joel Osment may have been seeing dead people, but you'll be seeing a lot of the city when you watch M. Night Shyamalan's *The Sixth Sense*, including scenes filmed on St. Albans Place, in St. Augustine Roman Catholic Church, and on Delancey Street.

49 OH, DEM GOLDEN SLIPPERS

What's the best way to celebrate a new year?

Every day is New Year's Day at the Mummers Museum.

Philadelphia has a long and beloved tradition of mummery. Considered the oldest folk festival in the country, the annual New Year's Mummers Parade dates back to January 1, 1901, and the tradition in the city actually began long before that. When immigrants from Scandinavia settled the area, they brought with them their holiday tradition of "Second Christmas," when people would visit their neighbors and continue the celebration. This evolved into the tradition—and the parade—we now know, which is part British Mummer play, part Feast of Saturnalia, part Florentine Carnival—and 100 percent Philadelphia.

Mummers are colorfully costumed entertainers who perform on the streets of Philadelphia (or in the Convention Center) on New Year's Day. There are six divisions (or types) of Mummers—the comics (clowns, usually well-liquored), the wench brigades (the newest addition, a breakaway from the comics), fancy (like comics, only fancier), fancy brigades (the "indoor" Mummers, who perform elaborate mini-musicals with elaborate sets and special effects), and the string bands (the live music division).

OH, DEM GOLDEN SLIPPERS

WHAT The Mummers Museum, a museum dedicated to the art of mummery

WHERE 1100 S. Second St., Philadelphia 19147

COST $5, includes guided tour

PRO TIP The museum has a free parking lot in the back. The gift shop is cash only.

Golden slippers are the most iconic image in mummery. String bands fill the streets on New Year's Day with the sounds of James Bland's song "Oh, Dem Golden Slippers," and the crowds sing and dance along. ©Mary Dixon Lebeau

Hundreds of thousands line the streets on New Year's Day to watch the Mummers Parade. If you can't be there January 1, however, you can visit the year-round Mummers Museum in South Philly. Opened in 1976 as part of the bicentennial celebration, the Mummers Museum showcases the history, the tradition, and the sheer pleasure of the Mummers, utilizing donated costumes, shared oral histories, videos, and audio to tell the Mummers' story.

An early parade is shown in black and white on a Mutophone, picture by picture. There are also costumes to try on—great for photo ops!—and films of the latest parade routines, plus a fun instructional display that teaches you how to do the Mummers' strut. Get your golden slippers ready!

Some Mummers utilize elaborate costuming, often costing thousands of dollars and some weighing in excess of one hundred pounds. For all the divisions, the cost of mummery far exceeds the prize money offered—but it isn't about the money anyway. All the preparation and work is done for the sheer love of mummery.

50

YOU SAY YOU WANT A REVOLUTION

What happened in the colonies after the Declaration of Independence was signed?

So . . . the colonists got together in 1776, declared independence from the British, rang the Liberty Bell, and all went home happy, right?

Of course not. The period between the early unrest of the 1760s and the creation of the Constitution in 1787 were messy years for the colonies, full of the birth pains necessary to bring forth our new democracy. These years are the focus of the Museum of the American Revolution, which opened a few blocks from Independence Hall on April 19, 2017—the anniversary date of the Battle of Lexington and Concord, the Revolution's first battle, on April 19, 1775.

Where the museum really shines is in its "deeper dig" into the stories of the colonists—not the Founding Fathers, the noted patriots, or the war heroes, but the everyday people who lived during this turbulent time. Seven displays include realistic life-size figures that bring history to life. One called "Resistance!" includes a two-story reproduction of the Liberty Tree, where colonists would meet to discuss the

---

The museum's vast collection allows visitors total immersion into the time period through a variety of films, audio presentations, and interactive opportunities. At the Battlefield Theater, for example, guests are taught to stand in ranks and move in formation before witnessing the Battle of Brandywine.

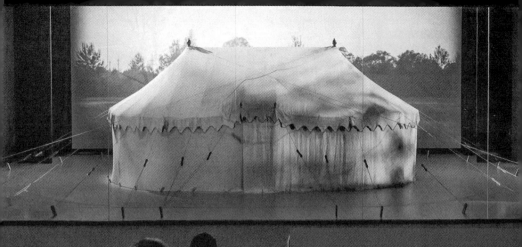

The war tent of General George Washington, where crucial decisions were made during the Revolutionary War, is a highlight of any visit to the Museum of the American Revolution. Photo courtesy Museum of the American Revolution.

WHAT Museum of the American Revolution

WHERE 101 S. Third St., Philadelphia 19106

COST $19; students, teachers, or military (with ID), $17; seniors, $17; youth six to eighteen, $12; children five or under, free. Tickets are good for two consecutive days.

PRO TIP An "any time" ticket, which allows immediate access to all exhibits without pre-booking a scheduled time, is available for $25. Joint tickets (allowing access to the National Constitution Center and the Museum of the American Revolution) are also available.

issues of the day. All the people of the time are represented, including women, Native Americans, and slaves, some of whom fought for the British.

Other memorable tableaus include a re-creation of Independence Hall, a display of an Oneida Indian council, and a large model of a privateer ship, which visitors can board. Approximately five hundred objects from the museum's collection are on display, including manuscripts and muskets, diaries, law books, and a pre-Revolutionary drum. The centerpiece of the collection is George Washington's Headquarters Tent, where the general who would become our first president lived and worked for most of the Revolutionary War.

51

THE SOUND OF MUSIC

Which top music acts had their roots in Philadelphia?

"Come on, baby, let's do the twist!"

Though he recorded a variety of dance records, Philadelphia's own Ernest Evans is best known for "The Twist," the dance sensation embraced by a generation. Recording under his stage name, Chubby Checker, Evans had 32 chart hits between 1962 and 1966; "The Twist" was so big that he even recorded a follow-up hit, "Let's Twist Again."

Until Dick Clark's death in 2012, he was known as "America's Oldest Living Teenager." He may have been born in New York, but Philadelphia embraced him as one of its own and closely followed his rise as the host of a little afternoon teen dance show called *Bandstand*.

Leopold Stokowski was the lauded long-term director of the Philadelphia Orchestra, a position he accepted in October 1912. He was a musical genius with a flair for the theatrical appreciated by aficionados, and he may be best

---

THE SOUND OF MUSIC

WHAT Philadelphia Music Alliance Walk of Fame

WHERE The Avenue of the Arts, Broad Street between Walnut and Spruce, Philadelphia 19107

COST Free

PRO TIP You can find the Walk of Fame outside Merriam Theater and the Academy of Music.

The Philadelphia Music Alliance is a grassroots not-for-profit dedicated to spreading awareness of and interest in the rich musical legacy of the city.

The Philadelphia Music Alliance Walk of Fame was established in 1986 to honor all those who made significant contributions to The Sound of Philadelphia (TSOP). Bill Haley, Mario Lanza, Bessie Smith, Bobby Rydell, and Dizzy Gillespie were all among the honorees during the Music Alliance Walk of Fame's inaugural year. ©Scott Lebeau

remembered by the masses as Walt Disney's collaborator on the film *Fantasia*.

Though each of these men made wildly different contributions to the world of music, they have one thing in common—all three, and eleven other men and women, were part of the initial class inducted into the Philadelphia Music Alliance Walk of Fame. Through the years, the Alliance has honored a variety of notables, including folk rocker Jim Croce (class of '88), super duo Hall and Oates ('93), female rocker Joan Jett ('96), and jazz artist Billie Holiday ('15). All made their mark in the world of music—and all had ties to Philadelphia.

Jazz and classical, rock and gospel, blues and soul—Philly has played a part in the development of all these styles, and each is represented on the Walk of Fame. Markers for each of the inductees can be found on the Walk of Fame on the Avenue of the Arts. The head marker is at the corner of Broad and Walnut streets.

52

CURIOUSER AND CURIOUSER

CURIOUSER AND CURIOUSER

WHAT The Mütter Museum

WHERE 19 S. Twenty-Second St., College of Physicians of Philadelphia, Philadelphia 19103

COST Adults, $18; seniors sixty-five and up, $16; military with ID, $15; students with ID and children six to seventeen, $13; children five and under, free

PRO TIP Yes, children five and under are free—but please, don't bring them. This place can be nightmare-inducing for the young (and the faint of heart). Strollers are not allowed in the museum. Neither are cameras, a rule that is strictly enforced. Lines are extremely long on Saturdays, so if you can choose a different day for your visit, you should.

What's the strangest thing a kid has ever swallowed?

If you are morbidly curious, you won't want to leave Philadelphia without a visit to the Mütter Museum.

Housed at the College of Physicians of Philadelphia, the Mütter displays an eclectic and amazing collection of eye-opening and jaw-dropping specimens, casts, skeletons, and slides, all with the goal of helping visitors gain a better understanding of the human body and disease. As its advertising promises, you will leave this museum "disturbingly informed."

How disturbing? Well, just take a look at the Chevalier Jackson Collection. In this enormous bureau are drawerfuls and drawerfuls of things people have actually inhaled or swallowed. These include safety pins, toy opera glasses, a battleship from the game Monopoly and six-pointed jacks. Ouch! Jackson, a renowned Philadelphia otolaryngologist, developed methods and tools for getting objects out of human

passageways—and used them quite often, as the collection numbers more than 2,300 pieces.

Other oddities on display include jars of baby fetuses, including a two-headed infant known as Jim and Joe; a wall of skulls; Broken Bodies, Empty Spirits, an exhibit detailing the history of medicine during the Civil War; a malignant tumor removed from President Grover Cleveland; and tissue from Lincoln assassin John Wilkes Booth. As you come in the doors, you'll find an exhibit detailing the Medical Oddities of Alice: Potions, Poisons, and Pathology, which considers the medical aspects of *Alice in Wonderland*.

Want more? Well, this is one of only two places in the world where you'll find pieces of Albert Einstein's brain (on slides). You can compare yourself to the tallest skeleton on display in America, or gape back at the Soap Lady, a wide-mouth corpse of a woman whose remains are encased in a fatty wax-like substance known as adipocere.

One of the most popular exhibits at the Mütter is the death cast and livers of twins Chang and Eng Bunker, who were born conjoined in Thailand in 1811. Following the twins' deaths in 1874, the autopsy of the brothers' bodies was performed at the College of Physicians of Philadelphia.

How are you like a jellybean?

On the third floor of the National Liberty Museum, visitors are confronted with a profound truth—in the form of two children made of jellybeans.

The sign accompanying the display reads, "Although they come in many different shades and sizes, every jellybean contains exactly the same ingredients inside. All human beings are also the same inside . . . just like me, just like you."

A visit to the National Liberty Museum, a newer addition to historic Old City, is all about encountering truth—the truth about our similarities despite our differences, and the truth that we can all be heroes, no matter who we are.

In the Inspiration exhibit, for example, visitors encounter a wall of pictures of famous Americans who have overcome adversity and can inspire us to do the same. The wall includes those you would expect, such as Helen Keller and Ray Charles, but also some surprises, including Brooke Shields and Donny Osmond.

More obstacles are explored in the permanent exhibit Voyage to Liberty, filled with stained-glass windows (reminding visitors of the religious persecution early Pilgrims fled), cut-glass figures, a glass chess set, and other

The centerpiece of the museum is the glass sculpture *Flame of Liberty*, by Dale Chihuly. The striking twenty-foot sculpture—as well as many other glass pieces in the museum—speaks to the strength and the fragility of liberty.

Kids love the jellybean people, a sweet lesson about how we're all the same inside. ©Scott Lebeau

artistic representations of how the human spirit can overcome adversity. On the same floor, Liberty Hall houses a collection of military medals, as well as an impressive display of White House china.

The theme of heroes resounds through the other floors. One exhibit, Heroes from Around the World, tells the stories of ordinary people who performed extraordinary acts in the pursuit of liberty. These include Nelson Mandela, locked away in a stark cell. The faces of two young girls peer out at visitors in the display honoring Anne Frank; the annex where she and her family hid from the Nazis can be viewed through a long, narrow peephole.

Another moving tribute to heroes is the Heroes of 9/11 Memorial, a three-story exhibit that includes a wall of Faces of Courage, each picture a hero who was killed as a result of the 2001 terrorist attack on our country.

54

COLLECTING THE STORIES

Can a museum inspire an appreciation for diversity?

Albert Einstein's pipe. Sandy Koufax's signed baseball. Steven Spielberg's camera and a piano belonging to Irving Berlin. Where can you find all these artifacts—and what do they have in common?

You can find all of these items and more on display at the National Museum of American Jewish History. The Smithsonian-affiliated museum is dedicated to the preservation and celebration of the impact of Jewish Americans, hoping this will inspire a greater appreciation for diversity.

The museum's core exhibition, displayed over three stories, illustrates the lives of Jewish immigrants as they made their way to America and settled here. As you explore the exhibition, you will come to know the people through the stories, the ideas, and the experiences they shared. Visitors gain a true appreciation for the trials immigrants face—from the time they first consider leaving their homeland through the process of assimilating in a new country, while holding onto their history, beliefs, and traditions.

To delve more deeply into American Jewish life, the museum's collections support the core exhibition and help make the stories come to life. It's here that you'll find a

COLLECTING THE STORIES

WHAT National Museum of American Jewish History

WHERE 101 S. Independence Mall East, Philadelphia 19106

COST Adults, $15; seniors (sixty-five and up), $13; children twelve and under and active military with ID, free

PRO TIP The Only in America® Gallery/Hall of Fame, located on the first floor, is free.

Along with celebrity artifacts, including Steven Spielberg's camera and Irving Berlin's piano, the museum also celebrates the everyday life of the American Jewish community through the ages. The collection includes a Yiddish typewriter, a Steiff teddy bear, and this notebook used by Eva Baen, a worker in a shirtwaist factory, to track her output circa 1914 to 1917 in Philadelphia. Photo used with the permission of the National Museum of American Jewish History.

tzedakah box, used to collect money for Jewish charities; a Jewish sampler stitched in 1813; a Hebrew alphabet learning board; bar and bat mitzvah cake toppers; a Yiddish typewriter; and much more.

You'll find exhibits commemorating the contributions of Albert Einstein, Steven Spielberg, Irving Berlin, and other notable Jewish Americans in the Only in America® Gallery/Hall of Fame. Spielberg's camera, Berlin's piano, and Koufax's ball . . . they're all in the hall.

But it's not all about memorabilia. The museum has an eye for the future, as well. Through a newer, digital initiative called Re:collection (recollection.nmajh.org), people can add their own stories, upload audio or video recordings, and post pictures. These can be shared and linked with others across the country.

The museum is open Wednesday through Sunday, as well as Tuesdays during special exhibitions, so it is closed most federal holidays. However, it is open on Martin Luther King Jr. Day, Presidents' Day, Independence Day, and Christmas Day. It is closed on several—but not all—of the traditional Jewish holidays. Check the museum's website for an up-to-date listing and to get a small discount on tickets purchased online.

55

WHERE PILGRIMS PRAY

Where can you view the relics of America's first male saint?

In modern times, very few people have been elevated to the status of saint by the Catholic Church. Yet the first canonized male in our country worked right here in Philadelphia, and his relics can be viewed by the religious and the curious in a shrine celebrating his life.

St. John Neumann came to America from Bohemia in 1836. He was ordained the fourth bishop of Philadelphia in 1852 and served in that capacity until his sudden death of a heart attack in 1860. During his work in this country, he founded the Catholic school system and built eighty-nine churches, as well as several orphanages and hospitals. He was canonized as a Catholic saint in 1977.

The shrine of St. John Neumann is in the lower church of St. Peter the Apostle Parish. A statue of the saint beckoning to a group of children is outside the building, making it easy to identify. Enter the site through the Fifth Street doors, where you'll find a museum and gift shop. Speak to a gift shop worker if you're interested in visiting the museum, which features exhibits relating to Neumann's life. It's usually only open Tuesday through Friday from 1:45 to 4:15 p.m. Of course, most people visit to see the remains of the saint, which can be viewed any day in the shrine.

In 2009, a fire at the shrine burned a wooden pulpit near the relics to ashes. However, the fire was contained to the pulpit, and the altar containing John Neumann's remains was unscathed.

John Neumann was a tireless preacher of the Gospel with a calling to serve the poor and disenfranchised. The body of this Roman Catholic saint lies under the main altar of the lower church of St. Peter the Apostle Church. The lower church was later renamed the National Shrine of St. John Neumann. ©Scott Lebeau

WHERE PILGRIMS PRAY

WHAT The National Shrine of St. John Neumann

WHERE 1019 N. Fifth St., Philadelphia 19123

COST Free

PRO TIP There are three free parking lots available to visitors to the shrine. Two have entrances off Lawrence Street, where you'll also find the St. John Neumann Center. One of these is also accessible from Fifth Street, as is the third lot. A free self-guided audio tour is available using your cellphone.

Going downstairs to the shrine (elevator available) feels like a descent into the catacombs. The shrine itself is expansive, framed with large stained-glass windows depicting the John Neumann story. Candles in red votives, long wooden pews, and the white runner across the altar make this feel like many other Catholic churches in the country—until you notice the saint's form enclosed in a clear case that makes up the base of the altar. Neumann's body, which was exhumed when he was canonized, is dressed in bishop's garb, and a mask mimicking his features in life covers his face.

129

56

EVERY TOMBSTONE TELLS A STORY

What Revolutionary War figure is commemorated in maple–on Pine?

He's now a noted patriot, but there was a time when John Adams wasn't sure declaring independence from England was the right move. He needed a little spiritual nudging, and he got it from Pastor George Duffield. Adams later shared with his wife, Abigail, that Duffield's sermon comparing King George to the Egyptian Pharaoh convinced him to sign the Declaration of Independence.

People have been inspired by sermons in the Old Pine Street Church since 1768. Originally known as the Third Presbyterian Church, it was designed by Colonial architect/builder Robert Smith. Today, it is still an active and vital church and the only pre-American Revolution Presbyterian church remaining in the city.

In 1777, the British conscripted the church for hospital use, using everything wooden in the building for fuel during their nine-month occupation. Since 1790, the edifice has undergone a series of architectural changes, the last in 1857 when an eighteen-foot-wide portico was added to the Pine

Philadelphia-based sculptor Roger Wing created the statue of George Duffield, who was the minister at Old Pine Street Church during the Revolutionary War. The likeness is carved from the trunk of a Norway maple tree. ©Scott Lebeau

Street side. Even with the changes, the church still stands on its original pre-Revolutionary foundation.

Duffield was the church's patriot pastor during the Revolution. At that time, he was also co-chaplain of the Continental Congress and lived with a fifty-pound bounty—dead or alive!—placed on him by King George III of England. His impassioned pleas against taxation without representation and for the cause of independence rallied his congregation, and Third Presbyterian became known as "the church of the patriots."

Duffield pastored the congregation here until his death in 1790. He is commemorated in the graveyard outside the church, his carved likeness rising up from a maple tree stump. In death, as in life, he looks as though he is preaching, this time to the 285 Revolutionary War soldiers who are buried next to their thirteen-star flags.

One revolutionary buried here is William Hurrie, who died in October 1781 at the age of sixty. According to the marker telling his story, Hurrie was the sexton and official bell ringer at Independence Hall. His constant bell ringing on July 8, 1776, summoned people to the State House lawn to hear the first public reading of the Declaration of Independence.

57 ONCE UPON A BENCH

ONCE UPON A BENCH

WHAT Once Upon a Nation Storytelling Benches, where storytellers share real stories about the city's historic district

WHERE Benches are located in the following places: Independence Visitor Center, Independence Square behind Independence Hall, Signers' Garden, Carpenters' Hall, the Powel House, the Museum of the American Revolution, Franklin Court, Christ Church, Elfreth's Alley, the Betsy Ross House, the Arch Street Meeting House, the National Constitution Center, and Franklin Square.

COST Free

PRO TIP The Storytelling Benches are seasonal, opening Memorial Day weekend, then Fridays and Saturdays until June 10. They open daily for the season Tuesdays through Saturdays between June 13 and August 12, then return to a Friday-Saturday schedule through Labor Day.

Can history really come alive for kids?

Philly has more history than a high school textbook—and sometimes that becomes a problem. The facts and figures may be fascinating, but they may not thrill the younger members of the family. Once they get beyond the Liberty Bell and the oldest-known American flag, kids may start losing interest in the historical elements of the city.

The solution is right on the curb—at the Once Upon a Nation Storytelling Benches. Thirteen of these charming benches are located throughout the historic area of the city, from Independence Visitor Center to Franklin Square and eleven stops in between. At each bench, a specially trained, costumed storyteller enthralls kids (and adults, as well) with a story about how history was made on the site.

The routine is the same from bench to bench: a story is told that somehow connects

The Once Upon a Nation Storytelling Bench at Franklin Square invites visitors to sit back and learn more about the historic sites of the city. ©Scott Lebeau

to the site where the bench is located. At their first bench, kids can pick up a flag, then collect a star from each storyteller they listen to. Upon completion, the flag can be redeemed for a ride on the Franklin Square Parx Liberty Carousel. Score!

The storytellers are as diverse as the stories they share. College students, middle-aged mothers, enthusiastic retirees, and more—all craft stories that leave young visitors glued to every word and wanting more. Fortunately, each storyteller is prepared with more than one story!

Feel free to interrupt and ask questions! The storytellers are extremely engaging and thoroughly prepared for whatever may be asked. This is a truly interactive experience.

⁵⁸ THE BIGGER, THE BETTER

Are our toys bigger than your toys?

If you're walking through Lenfest Plaza in our fair city and happen upon an oversized paintbrush tilted as though it's about to coat you with red paint, you may just wonder where it came from.

Ditto the giant button, split down the middle, that you encounter while roaming the campus of the University of Pennsylvania. And what's up with the huge clothespin standing outside City Hall, in the shadow of Billy Penn's statue?

Well, these sculptures all came from the mind of Swedish-American artist Claes Oldenburg. Either alone or, in the case of *Split Button*, together with his wife Coosje van Bruggen, Oldenburg created these blown-up replicas of everyday household items—and with them, added a touch of whimsy to our busy city.

Take, for instance, *Paint Torch*, which stands almost fifty-one feet high and is situated at a sixty-degree diagonal off the street, poised on the point of the brush's handle.

Clothespin and *Split Button* were created with funding from the Philadelphia Redevelopment Authority's Percent for Art Program. Since 1959, developers who build on land acquired by the PRA are required to spend at least 1 percent of the construction costs on site-specific works of art. Hundreds of works of public art now installed in the city are the result of the Percent for Art Program.

A jumbo top hat is just one of the oversized Monopoly and other game pieces that make up Your Move, *a larger-than-life whimsical view of the games people play.* ©Scott Lebeau

The sculpture, complete with a six-foot blob of paint on the sidewalk nearby, is a fitting celebration of the nearby Pennsylvania Academy of the Fine Arts.

Or consider *Clothespin,* Oldenburg's 1976 creation of COR-TEN steel with a stainless-steel spring. Kids these days may not even know what a clothespin is, but my grandmother used to hang clothes in her backyard, and this sculpture is reminiscent of the wooden clips she would use to hold our clean sheets on the line. Only bigger, shinier, and more stylized, of course.

But Oldenburg isn't the only artist thinking big in Philadelphia. If you visit LOVE Park, go across the street to the Municipal Services Building Plaza, where you'll find giant Monopoly pieces, jumbo dominos, and oversized checkerboard pieces. This is *Your Move* by Daniel Martinez, Renee Petropoulos, and Roger White, installed here in 1996.

THE ORIGINAL CHEESESTEAK WARS

Where did the cheesesteak originate?

If Pat Olivieri hadn't grown tired of hot dogs for lunch, the culinary world as we know it in Philly might have been very different.

Olivieri, who operated a hot dog cart back in 1930 with his brother Harry, did grow tired of his daily noontime frank. Trying to come up with something new, Pat sent Harry to a local butcher for some scrap meat. He cooked the meat on their hot dog grill, sliced it up and added onions, then piled it into a roll.

Thus, the steak sandwich was born.

Following a friend's advice, Olivieri eliminated dogs from the menu and opened Pat's King of Steaks at Ninth and Wharton. It wasn't until the fifties, though, when employees and customers demanded cheese on the sandwich, that an icon was born.

The success of Pat's could only mean one thing: others would try to duplicate his sandwich. Imitators can be found on almost every street corner in Philly (and quite a few on the Jersey side of the bridge, as well), but the "real competition" in the cheesesteak world is Geno's

The rivalry between the shops may be beefed up, but it certainly hasn't hurt either side. Oh, and another Rocky reference—in the original Rocky, Rocky's boss (a loan shark, natch!) takes the Italian Stallion to Pat's for a cheesesteak.

Right across the street, Geno's Steaks is Pat's closest—but far from only—rival. The good-natured Cheesesteak Wars have been battled out 24/7 since 1966. ©Scott Lebeau

THE ORIGINAL CHEESESTEAK WARS

WHAT Pat's King of Steaks and Geno's Steaks

WHERE The corners of Ninth Street and Passyunk Avenue, South Philadelphia

COST Depends on what you order—you can usually get a cheesesteak for around ten bucks

PRO TIP The sandwiches are delicious—and huge! To compare, buy one from each corner and then share with friends!

Steaks—right across the street from Pat's, at the intersection of Ninth and Passyunk in South Philly.

"I figured if you want to sell a steak, go where they're eating them," said owner Joe Vento, who opened Geno's in 1966. Competitors gave him six months, but for more than fifty years, Geno's and Pat's have been battling the cheesesteak war, seven days a week, twenty-four hours a day.

The friendly competition doesn't seem to hurt either proprietor, as lines start forming in the late morning and hold strong throughout the day at both locations. In both restaurants, customers cozy up to the order window to request a steak "wit" or "witout" (onions, of course) and to specify their all-important cheese preference. Connoisseurs swear by Cheez Whiz, but provolone and American cheese are also popular choices.

Where can you come face to face with a sphinx?

When you're surrounded by as many historical firsts as you are in Philadelphia, it's easy to think of the city as very, very old. Then you come face to face with a sphinx, and you realize that, in the scheme of things, Philadelphia is a relative newcomer.

The Sphinx of Ramses II of the Nineteenth Dynasty (circa 1293-1185 BCE!) is the headliner in the Egypt (Sphinx) Gallery, one of the many signature galleries at the University of Pennsylvania Museum of Archaeology and Anthropology (or, as it is more commonly known, the Penn Museum). Surrounding the impressive thirteen-ton sphinx are artifacts from the palace built for New Kingdom Pharaoh Merenptah (1213-1204 BCE), the best-preserved royal palace ever excavated in Egypt.

A second gallery dedicated to the same area is the Egypt (Mummies) Gallery, where you'll find coffin stones, mummy masks, and other Egyptian sculptures. The centerpiece here is the seated statue of Ramses II in all his imposing splendor. But notice how his head's a little small for his body? Here's a secret: It's believed that the statue was originally carved in the late Middle Kingdom. It was later usurped from the earlier ruler and reconstructed using Ramses's head.

The Egypt Galleries are amazing, but so are the other wonders to be found at the Penn Museum. The museum

The Penn Museum, considered one of the world's finest archeological and anthropological museums, was founded in 1878. It is the largest university museum in the country.

This seated limestone statue of Ramses II of Herakleopolis, Egypt, circa 1250 BCE, is featured in the Egypt (Mummies) Gallery at the Penn Museum. Photo by Thomas A. Stanley and used courtesy of the Penn Museum.

is considered one of the world's finest, and its collection numbers nearly a million objects. It's a working museum that has sponsored worldwide expeditions for more than a century. Special exhibitions in recent years have included Moundbuilders: Ancient Architects of North America, Magic in the Ancient World, and The Golden Age of King Midas, while permanent exhibits showcase such wonders as a sixth-century Buddha, tablets inscribed with cuneiform, African nail fetish figures, and terra-cotta temple ornaments from Etruscan Italy.

61 PERFORMING AN OPERATION

Where is America's oldest operating theater?

In a world where hand sanitizer is in every purse, on every desk, and at the entrance of every supermarket, it's hard to fathom the sanitary conditions during surgery in the 1800s. Or, more appropriately, the lack of sanitary conditions—because there weren't any, unless you count the sawdust spread on the floor the day of a surgery to soak up the blood.

Surgeries as they were performed from 1804 through 1868 in the Surgical Amphitheatre at Pennsylvania Hospital weren't for the faint of heart. First of all, prior to the introduction of ether in 1846, no medical anesthesia was provided at all. The best the patient could hope for was enough liquor to squelch the pain or a tap on the head with a mallet to knock him out prior to being strapped onto the operating table especially fitted for the human form. Surgeons, who washed their hands only after the procedure, would lecture throughout the

---

PERFORMING AN OPERATION

WHAT America's oldest existing surgical amphitheater

WHERE Pennsylvania Hospital, 800 Spruce St., Philadelphia 19107

COST Suggested donation of $5 a person; tours are guided and should be scheduled forty-eight hours in advance.

PRO TIP Surgeries were performed on the third floor, but not to hide the cries of the patients. The real reason was the natural light that flowed through the windows on the ceiling of this circular room. Many surgeons still say that natural light is the best to operate by—but at the time, it limited surgeries to between the hours of 11 a.m. and 2 p.m. on sunny days, because there was no electricity.

The country's oldest existing surgical amphitheater is on the third floor at Pennsylvania Hospital. Early nineteenth-century surgeries were performed in this room to an audience of medical students and other interested ticketholders. Photo by Robert Neroni and used courtesy of the Pennsylvania Hospital Historic Collections.

operation to an audience made up of medical students and any other interested parties. Operations, which were less frequent than they are today, were advertised events. Tickets were sold to those who were free in the middle of the day and had the money.

Founded in 1751, Pennsylvania Hospital is the nation's first chartered hospital. Today it's still a working hospital, bustling with dedicated doctors and nurses who all wash up prior to caring for their patients. But on the third floor of the historic Pine Building, the country's oldest surgical amphitheater still exists—and is open to visitors as part of a guided historic tour of the building, which also includes the Historic Library, Great Court, Gallery Pavilion, and, weather permitting, the Physic Garden.

Pennsylvania Hospital is part of the University of Pennsylvania. It was founded twenty-five years before the American Revolution by a group of public citizens inspired by a philosophy of caring. Not surprisingly, Benjamin Franklin was one of the founders. The hospital has always been nondenominational, but it had a heavy Quaker influence for the first one hundred years.

What was the curse of Billy Penn?

Situated on the exact center of William Penn's 1682 plans for the city (a spot known as Centre Square), Philadelphia City Hall is the nation's largest municipal building. All three branches of city and county government have a presence here, working on policy in the building's almost seven hundred rooms. City Hall was designed by Scottish architect John McArthur Jr.; work on the building began in 1871 and was completed in 1901. Besides its great functionality, the building is an architectural masterpiece. Designed in the French Second Empire tradition, it is a square around a central public courtyard.

McArthur intended the building to be the tallest structure in the world, but both the Eiffel Tower and the Washington Monument were completed first—and were taller. Still, those were not functional, inhabitable buildings, so City Hall was the tallest occupied structure in the world until the Metropolitan Life Building opened in New York in 1909.

The William Penn statue is the tallest statue on top of any building in the world. Ironically, the real Penn would not be pleased about the statue because, as a Quaker, he did not believe in "graven images."

Maybe it was always cursed? Construction on the building took thirty years, following numerous delays and financial overruns. The building cost more than $24 million to build. Opposite: Even on dark days, it's easy to spot the statue of William Penn on top of the Philadelphia City Hall. Penn laid out the plan for the building's spot two hundred years before it was built. ©Scott Lebeau

More important to residents, though, is that City Hall remained the tallest in Philadelphia until 1987. A gentleman's agreement forbade any construction in the city higher than the brim of the hat of William Penn, the thirty-seven-foot-tall statue on top of City Hall. The agreement was broken in 1987, with the construction of One Liberty Place, which, at sixty-one stories, was 397 feet taller than City Hall.

Thus began the supposed Curse of Billy Penn. None of the city's four major sports franchises won a championship from that date on. The drought went on for more than twenty years. Then, in June 2007, a 5.2-inch statuette of Penn was attached to the final beam placed in the fifty-eight-story Comcast Center, returning the city founder to his "top spot." In October 2008—one year and four months later—the Phillies won the World Series.

CENTRE SQUARE

WHAT Philadelphia City Hall, a National Historic Landmark

WHERE Broad and Market streets, Philadelphia 19107

COST Visiting the building is free. Two guided tours are available and cost as follows: City Hall Tower Tour—adults, $8; seniors, students, youth, and military, $6; children under three, free; City Hall Interior Tour (includes tower)—adults, $15; seniors over sixty-five and military, $10; students/youth, $8; children under three, free

PRO TIP There is a viewing tower below the statue, approximately 484 feet above the ground. A stop here is included in the tours.

63

THE PHILADELPHIA STORY

Where can you find the biggest walkable map of the city?

The Liberty Bell. Independence Hall. The Declaration of Independence and the US Constitution.

Because Philadelphia played such a big part in the history of our country, we sometimes forget that the city has a history of its own. Fortunately, we have a museum of our own to remind us whence we came. And it's due, in a big way, to inventor and radio pioneer A. Atwater Kent.

Back in 1938, Kent purchased an elegant Greek Revival structure that had been the original home of the Franklin Institute. Kent gave the site to the city to use as a museum for Philadelphia history. There was one other stipulation— the museum had to bear his name. Called the Atwater Kent Museum since its inception in 1941, the museum was renamed the Philadelphia History Museum at the Atwater Kent in 2010.

Today, the museum successfully unites Philadelphia's rich history with its prominence in everyday life circa the twenty-first century. Where else can you find the wampum belt given by the Lenni Lenape tribe to the Penn family— symbolizing peaceful relations—within eyeshot of the boxing gloves Philadelphian Joe Frazier wore during his victory over Muhammed Ali in what was dubbed "the Fight of the Century"?

History is alive, and ever changing, at the Philadelphia History Museum. That's because the museum's collection numbers more than 100,000 objects dating back to the 1680s. While some exhibitions are permanent, others are currently being rotated in and out.

South Street

THE PHILADELPHIA STORY

WHAT The Philadelphia History Museum at the Atwater Kent

WHERE 15 S. Seventh St., Philadelphia 19106

COST General admission, $10; seniors, $8; students and teens, $6; children under twelve and active military, free

PRO TIP The designer of the building, John Haviland, was also the architect of Eastern State Penitentiary. Apparently, he could design for all types!

YOU ARE HERE . . . At the Philadelphia History Museum at the Atwater Kent, a street map of the city fills the Main Gallery floor. It's the world's largest walkable map of Philly. ©Mary Dixon Lebeau
Inset: These iron shackles were once used in the transport of slaves from Africa, who were first brought to Philadelphia in 1684. According to the display at the Philadelphia History Museum, William Penn preferred enslaved Africans to indentured white servants because the slaves "worked for life." ©Scott Lebeau

The permanent exhibition Face to Facebook explores how the people of Philadelphia have pictured themselves from the seventeenth century through the present day. Make sure to join the portrait gallery yourself by taking your own picture behind the portrait gallery frame, then emailing it to the museum for inclusion on its website.

But the "can't miss" attraction at the museum is the world's largest walkable map of Philadelphia, which fills the museum's Main Gallery floor. Natives can find their own street address throughout the city and even in nearby Jersey, while visitors can use worksheets to locate historical sites throughout the city.

64

BUTTERFLIES ARE FREE TO FLY

So, what bugs you?

The Insectarium is not new to Philadelphia. The museum opened in 1992, when a local exterminator began showing off his catches in repurposed fish tanks. The curious came, and the museum grew. In 2017, and the museum changed ownership, and the Insectarium has been rebranded as the Philadelphia Insectarium and Butterfly Pavilion.

Now owned by entomologist John Cambridge, the vibe is more educational, more scientific, than it was in its previous incarnations, and yet the museum maintains its sense of fun. After all, what could be more joyful than discovering the unseen but thoroughly successful world of those little creatures who share our planet? A visit to the IBP may include walking through a giant interactive beehive, encountering a Goliath centipede, or mustering up the courage it takes to hold a friendly tarantula. The museum also boasts the most diverse living praying mantis collection on the East Coast. And there's more than just insects. IBP is also home to a variety of spiders, fish, amphibians, and reptiles.

BUTTERFLIES ARE FREE TO FLY

WHAT The Philadelphia Insectarium and Butterfly Pavilion

WHERE 8046 Frankford Ave., Philadelphia 19136

COST Adults, $11.95; children, $9.95; seniors, students, teachers, police, firefighters, and military (with ID), $9.95; infants/toddlers, free

PRO TIP Free parking is available in a lot next to the building. Metered street parking is also available. The building is three stories, with a café on the ground floor.

Make friends with a tarantula—if you have the nerve—at the Philadelphia Insectarium and Butterfly Pavilion. The magical world of metamorphosis is celebrated in the Butterfly Pavilion, where visitors can see butterflies emerge from the chrysalis stage. ©Scott Lebeau

A highlight of the visit is the recently opened Butterfly Pavilion. The seven-thousand-square-foot display is one of the largest in North America, costing $1.2 million. Thousands of butterflies, both local and exotic, call the beautiful tropical ecosphere home. Here you can watch a butterfly free itself of its chrysalis and get ready to fly. And fly they do, often landing on unsuspecting but delighted visitors. But be prepared—the pavilion is kept at a balmy eighty degrees.

According to the staff, the museum also features the world's largest ferrofluid fountain, a visual aid in the Butterfly Pavilion that allows visitors to use magnets to control the flow of water, paralleling the way monarch butterflies are controlled during migration by the magnetic field of the Earth.

An interactive touchscreen monitor teaches visitors about butterfly anatomy. Made just for the pavilion, it is the largest touchscreen in North America.

65

ARTISTIC REFLECTIONS

Where do random pieces come together to form beauty?

Bicycle wheels. Broken mirrors. Random doll parts. Discarded tiles.

Is it true that one man's junk is another man's art? The answer is a resounding yes on Philly's South Street. In fact, the intersection of haphazard and whimsy in Philadelphia's Magic Gardens is more than just artistic—it's, well, magical.

More than an art gallery, Philadelphia's Magic Gardens is the glittering vision of artist Isaiah Zagar, who created the mosaics in the garden and along South Street. He and his wife, Julia, were major contributors to the revitalization of the area in the sixties, and his work has appeared on the street and throughout the city since that time. Some thirty years later, in 1994, Zagar began designing the garden, working with layers of found objects on fences he put up around vacant lots. The creativity couldn't be contained, and the art spilled out over the emptiness of the lots. Then, in 2002, the property owner decided to sell the lots and demanded that the mosaics be dismantled.

But here's where some urban magic comes in. The community embraced the eclectic art environment and refused to see it dismantled. A two-year legal battle ensued,

---

Isaiah Zagar's folk art is also a staple at Eye's Gallery, which he and his wife, Julia, established in 1964, soon after they finished a stint with the Peace Corps. Another South Street favorite, Eye's Gallery features three stories of handpicked fair-trade jewelry, fashion, and folk art.

The folk art wonderland of mirrors and tile is the lifework of artist Isaiah Zagar. And it may take a lifetime to discover its secrets. ©Scott Lebeau

but in the end the not-for-profit organization Philadelphia's Magic Gardens, dedicated to the preservation of the artwork on the site, was incorporated.

Philadelphia's Magic Gardens opened to the public in 2008. Today, it's especially popular with the Instagram set, but this space is so much more. Wander the mosaic maze and find yourself lost in the mystery of broken pieces, the beauty of what remains behind.

ARTISTIC REFLECTIONS

WHAT Philadelphia's Magic Gardens, three city blocks featuring inside art galleries and an outdoor mosaic labyrinth

WHERE 1022-1024 South St., Philadelphia 19147

COST Timed general admission tickets: adults, $10; seniors and students, $8; children six to twelve, $5; children five and under, free

PRO TIP It's best to buy tickets online to secure your visit time. Guided tours are also available at an additional cost. Check the calendar on the website for tour times and special events.

66

TALES FROM THE CRYPT

What's the liveliest contemporary art site in the city?

Considering the roots of the space it currently occupies, it may be ironic to say that PhilaMOCA has brought the underground performance art scene to life in Philadelphia.

PhilaMOCA—or the Philadelphia Mausoleum of Contemporary Art—is a vibrant showcase for the best the city has to offer in alternative art. Playing host to more than 250 events a year (ranging from Saturday morning cartoons to underground/alternative film screenings and from a Music Video Book Club to live comedy acts and fashion shows), PhilaMOCA provides a creative outlet for up-and-coming local performers while bringing in thought-provoking and exciting artists from all over. It's part stage, part gallery, always edgy, and always alive.

But why "mausoleum"? What is that about? PhilaMOCA is housed in the historic Finney & Son Building, a former mausoleum and tombstone showroom dating back to 1865. So you can say the avant-garde art scene resurrected this space.

After the mausoleum business closed in the sixties, the building remained vacant for more than twenty years. A sculptor lived there briefly in the eighties, but the space didn't really come alive until local music producer Diplo bought the building in the early years of the twenty-first century and used it as the home base of the Mad Decent record label. PhilaMOCA was established here in 2010.

With more than a century of creepy history, PhilaMOCA brings a fun and unique spin to the modern-day art gallery. PhilaMOCA exterior photo by Justin Roman, courtesy PhilaMOCA. Inset: PhilaMOCA has established its reputation as the go-to venue for fresh art, eye-opening performances, and freaky fun. PhilaMOCA Mondo Mausoleum Party by Arin Sang-urai, courtesy PhilaMOCA.

TALES FROM THE CRYPT

WHAT PhilaMOCA (Philadelphia Mausoleum of Contemporary Art)

WHERE 531 N. Twelfth St., Philadelphia 19123

COST Varies, depending on the performance. Check the calendar on the website for details.

PRO TIP Free parking is readily available on Spring Garden Street (the nearest intersecting street) and on other surrounding blocks.

The Mausoleum is located in the Eraserhood, the unflinchingly industrial area in North Philly where artist and filmmaker David Lynch lived. PhilaMOCA also holds an annual celebration of Lynch's career as a filmmaker and artist known as Eraserhood Forever (And Ever). Each April, it also hosts the annual two-and-a-half-week Cinedelphia, a celebration of rarities, alternative films, and cult classics, many with a tie to Philly.

67 GIVE PIZZA CHANCE

In a city known for cheesesteaks, does pizza have any significance?

Philadelphians cannot live on cheesesteaks alone. Thus, we have our pizza. You can find crowded pizzerias in every Philly neighborhood. So what sets Pizza Brain, the tiny Fishtown establishment, apart?

Well, the secret here isn't the pizza, which is a delicious artisan thin crust, available with a variety of toppings in appealingly curious combinations. All good, but pretty well-known. What's secret about Pizza Brain is that it holds the distinction of being the world's first pizza museum and the curator of the largest collection of pizza memorabilia. The restaurant even has the Guinness World Record certificate to prove it.

Now, don't be led astray. Philadelphia is renowned for museums such as the Franklin Institute, the Philadelphia Museum of Art, and the Please Touch Museum. Pizza Brain's Museum of Pizza Culture does not number among such giants, but it certainly holds its own in kitschy fun.

Think of it more as an extensive personal collection, displayed throughout Pizza Brain and the adjacent attached building, home of Little Baby's Ice Cream. Because that's pretty much what it is. Guinness certified the collection in 2011, before Pizza Brain became an LLC, so it is listed

Places like this give new meaning to "hole in the wall." The pizzeria looks like it was literally carved into a brick wall. Don't expect a "pizza chain" atmosphere. This place is genuine, and I mean that in all the best ways.

Everything pizza! Here you'll find vinyl copies of "The Pizza Song," clocks with pepperoni slices under each number, a pizza-tossing Barbie, and artwork of the Founding Fathers sharing a pie. ©Scott Lebeau

GIVE PIZZA CHANCE

WHAT Pizza Brain, the world's first pizza museum

WHERE 2313 Frankford Ave., Philadelphia 19125

COST The museum is free—but you won't be able to resist dropping some dough in Pizza Brain, the restaurant where the memorabilia is displayed.

PRO TIP Parking is available on the street, and it's free (now there's a rarity!). It's a cash-only establishment.

as the individual collection of Kensington-based artist Brian Dwyer, a principal of the company.

Everywhere you look, you'll find something pizza related. Not quite a museum, but certainly extensive, and totally fun. There is a plethora of those pizza-sustained Teenage Mutant Ninja Turtles, a few Domino's Noids, a Pizza Drop Plinko game, and walls full of pictures, posters, marketing material, and pizza boxes.

THE POLISH PROVISION

THE POLISH PROVISION

WHAT Polish American Cultural Center Museum and Thaddeus Kosciuszko National Memorial, museums memorializing the contributions of the Polish to American history

WHERE Polish American Cultural Museum—308 Walnut St., Philadelphia 19106; Thaddeus Kosciuszko National Memorial—301 Pine St., Philadelphia 19106

COST Free

PRO TIP The Thaddeus Kosciuszko National Memorial is run by the National Park Service and is only open seasonally on weekends April through October.

Which Revolutionary heroes were Polish?

More than a million people crowded Logan Square when the Polish Pontiff, Pope John Paul II, said mass there in 1979. The pope, certainly, was beloved—but he wasn't the only Polish hero admired by those in Philadelphia.

Two Polish military men joined with the colonists during the Revolutionary War. One, nobleman Casimir Pulaski, is considered one of the founders of the American cavalry. Recruited by the Marquis de Lafayette and Benjamin Franklin, Pulaski was referred to General George Washington. He arrived in Philadelphia in 1777 and joined Washington's troops at Brandywine. In the following year, when

Another hero from the Philly area with Polish roots is John Cardinal Krol, the archbishop of Philadelphia from 1961 to 1988. He was the first Polish American to be ordained an archbishop. Krol was present for the canonization of his predecessor, Bishop John Neumann.

Washington formed an American cavalry, Pulaski was put in charge. He was fatally wounded by a cannonball in 1779.

The other, Thaddeus Kosciuszko, was a brilliant military engineer who assisted with the defeat of the British at Saratoga in 1777. He also designed fortifications used by the colonists during the war, including one at West Point. Kosciuszko eventually returned to Poland to assist in his country's own revolution against Russia. He came back to Philly in 1797, taking up residence in the house on Pine Street that is now the Thaddeus Kosciuszko National Memorial. Here, visitors can see many of Kosciuszko's military innovations, watch a film (in English or Polish!) about his life and career, and see the period artifacts in his late-eighteenth-century bedchamber.

Learn more about both men—and the contributions of Polish Americans to both the area and the country—at the Polish American Cultural Center Museum, just a short walk away. In the Exhibit Hall, visitors can enjoy Polish folk art, including hand-painted Easter eggs. There are also exhibits featuring Marie Curie, Nicolaus Copernicus, and, of course, Pope John Paul II.

No museum dedicated to the Polish experience would be complete without some reference to the Polish Pope, John Paul II, who was beloved by the Catholics in Philadelphia and worldwide. When he visited the city in 1979, Pope John Paul II held mass, attended by more than a million people, in Logan Circle. ©Mary Dixon Lebeau

FRAMEWORK FOR FREEDOM

What does an executive mansion teach about slavery?

Way back when the country was new, Philadelphia was the nation's capital. And from 1790 to 1800, presidents George Washington and John Adams lived not on Pennsylvania Avenue but in Pennsylvania itself, at the nation's executive mansion on Market Street, appropriately known as the President's House.

The three-story house no longer stands—the main home was demolished in 1852, and the surviving sections of the building were taken down in the 1950s when Independence Mall was created. But in late 2000, some of the house's foundation was uncovered while the area was being prepared for the Liberty Bell Center. It was discovered that the center would be within walking distance of Washington's slaves' quarters.

Obviously, the contradiction of a slaveowner as the leader of this land of liberty didn't go unnoticed. Now a memorial, the site is known as President's House: Freedom and Slavery in the Making of a New Nation, and it tells the story not only

---

Two of the nine slaves who served Washington in the President's House eventually escaped. One of them, Ona (or Oney) Judge, escaped from Philadelphia to New Hampshire. Washington made several attempts to get the seamstress back, but New Hampshire officials assisted Judge, who remained free until her death in 1848.

The information in the exhibit broadens the understanding of the people who had a role in the early days of our country—including those of African descent, both free and enslaved. ©Scott Lebeau

FRAMEWORK FOR FREEDOM

WHAT The President's House

WHERE 600 Market St., Philadelphia 19106

COST Free

PRO TIP You can see fragments of the original house displayed in a glass case. While living here, Washington signed the Fugitive Slave Act, making it a criminal act to assist a slave in escaping or to obstruct his recapture.

of the two presidents who lived in the house but also of the nine slaves who served Washington there.

There is no building—just an open-air brick structure that allows glimpses of the original foundation. The history of the house, as well as descriptions of the roles slaves played in Washington's executive mansion and in our country, is told on signs and in videos throughout the structure. The exhibit is self-guided and can be read and absorbed at your own pace.

THE CORNERSTONE OF REBELLION

WHAT The dedication stone at the Free Quaker Meeting House

WHERE 320 Arch St., Philadelphia 19106

COST Free

PRO TIP The dedication stone is tough to photograph, as the elements have taken their toll on the inscription. Still, it is visible to the naked eye (at least for those with twenty-twenty vision). A path behind the Meeting House leads to the Independence Visitor Center.

Where were the Friends fighting–and what were they fighting about?

The American Revolution presented a problem for the Religious Society of Friends (also known as the Quakers) living in Philadelphia at that time. That's because Quakers are pacifists. A tenet of the Friends' faith is the Peace Testimony, also known as the testimony against war, which states that Friends will promote peace and refuse to bear arms in times of conflict.

Of course, Philadelphia was a city designed by William Penn, a Quaker, and had a large population of Friends living within its borders. Some were loyal to England, while others supported the colonists' stand. In either case, the majority followed the Peace Testimony and tried not to get involved.

Not so, though, for the Free Quakers. These Friends were also known as the Fighting Quakers because they answered the call for people to fight in the colonial militia. They believed the cause of the Revolution was too important to be ignored. These Friends were "read out of meeting"—or shunned by their church for their support of the Revolution.

The Free (or "Fighting") Quakers met at the Free Quaker Meeting House after being disowned by their own congregations for supporting the Revolutionary War effort, which was against the Quaker tradition of pacifism. Inset: Although most of the building is original, the Free Quaker Meeting House has been moved from its original location. Because of the widening of the street, the entire structure was moved north and west. ©Scott Lebeau

Approximately two hundred of these expelled Friends opened their own house of worship on a corner on Arch Street in 1783, calling it the Free Quaker Meeting House. It was used until 1834, when lack of attendance forced its two remaining members—Betsy Ross and John Price Wetherill—to close its doors.

The building is open to visitors on weekends, but perhaps the most compelling aspect of the structure is always accessible. At the top of the building above the front door, look for the dedication stone. It is a white rectangle that reads, "By General Subscription for the FREE QUAKERS erected in the YEAR of OUR LORD 1783 of the EMPIRE 8." Written five years before the Constitution, the stone may indicate the way the people of the time were thinking about their future nation.

If you tour the inside, you'll see some original furniture, as well as an original window. There's also an exhibit of the tissue pattern Free Quaker Betsy Ross used in making the five-pointed star on the American flag.

THIS LITTLE PIGGY WENT TO MARKET

Where's the city's favorite piggy bank?

Children visiting Reading Terminal Market with their parents may ask for a coin to feed to Philbert the Pig, the market's three-foot-tall bronze mascot. Philbert—whose name is a play on nearby Filbert Street, but spelled in the style of Philadelphia, the Phillies, and the Phanatic—is actually a piggy bank who can be fed bills or coins through his mouth. (There's also a slot on his clear cashbox platform, for those who wish to donate in a more traditional way.) Funds usually benefit the Food Trust, although other charitable causes are often beneficiaries of Philbert's "meals" as well.

Reading Terminal Market is an enclosed public market that opened its doors in 1893 after public opinion and city law began to turn against outdoor markets, which were considered unsanitary and unsafe. Occupying space that was previously used by the Reading Railroad Company, Reading Terminal Market is now home to nearly eighty independently owned small businesses, most of them food

---

The market seems to reinvent itself regularly, with pop-up food carts, distilleries, chocolatiers, and corn dog vendors now showing up between the butcher shops and bakeries. But the old staples still thrive—one popular vendor, Bassetts Ice Cream, has been at Reading Terminal since 1893.

When it opened in February 1893, the street-level market shook whenever trains roared overhead. By 1913, 250 food vendors and one hundred farmers had stalls in Reading Terminal Market. ©Scott Lebeau

related. Visitors to the market can choose freshly butchered meat, sample artisan cheeses, take home a sack of fresh produce, and stop for a cup of coffee and a cookie before heading home. The market is the epitome of "something for everyone," featuring candy stores, soap vendors, flower shops, and housewares.

But the focus here is food. A variety of food vendors and delicatessens can satisfy any appetite, offering freshly made fudge, a variety of local and imported beers, piping hot soft pretzels, pizza, and sandwiches such as cheesesteaks and pulled pork (sorry, Philbert).

72 HIS WHOLE LIFE WAS A MILLION-TO-ONE SHOT

HIS WHOLE LIFE WAS A MILLION-TO-ONE SHOT

WHAT *Rocky* sites, places of note to fans of Sylvester Stallone's series of movies about boxer Rocky Balboa

WHERE The *Rocky* steps, statue, and Sylvester Stallone's footprints: Philadelphia Museum of Art, 2600 Benjamin Franklin Pkwy., Philadelphia 19130; Adrian's gravesite: Laurel Hill Cemetery, 3822 Ridge Ave., Philadelphia 19132

COST Free

PRO TIP *Rocky* is still big business in Philly, with a variety of guided *Rocky* tours available throughout the city.

Where is Rocky's wife buried?

Yo, Adrian! Visitors to our city have been looking for Rocky Balboa ever since the rags-to-riches story hit the big screen in 1976 (and captured the Best Picture Oscar for the year). Yes, we're talking about *Rocky*, the little movie that could. Local lore has it that an unknown Sylvester Stallone, who wrote the script in three days, turned down lucrative offers for his story because he didn't want anyone other than himself in the lead role.

Rocky was made on a shoestring budget of just over $1 million and became the highest-grossing film of 1976. It also brought quite a bit of attention to Philly, as people clamored to check out the pet stores, beat up on the beef, and, of course, run up the steps just like Rocky did.

Now almost every visitor to the city wants to run the *Rocky* steps. They're actually the steps of the Philadelphia

162

Left: Once outside the now-razed Spectrum arena, the Rocky statue can be found at the base of the Philadelphia Museum of Art steps, where he famously ended his workout. ©Max Weidler

Right: Yo, Adrian! In between Rocky V *and the release of* Rocky Balboa, *Rocky's leading lady dies of ovarian cancer. Rocky is seen making visits to her gravesite, which is located in Laurel Hill Cemetery. Her tombstone can still be found there—the only one for a fictional character in the distinguished graveyard. ©Mary Dixon Lebeau*

Museum of Art. These steps are one of the most iconic movie locations of all time, because everyone remembers Rocky's run to the top during training.

Conveniently located at the bottom of the stairs is the statue of Rocky Balboa created for *Rocky III*. Get your picture taken with the bronze image of Sylvester Stallone in his most famous role.

Almost anyone in Philly can point you to these two *Rocky* landmarks—but here's one that's not so well known. If you visit Laurel Hill Cemetery, you can find—among the sad statues and eerie memorials—the burial place of Adrian Balboa, Rocky's beloved wife. Adrian's grave was featured in *Rocky Balboa*, and the heavy granite gravestone used in the movie is still on display near the main office.

Paulie Pennino, Rocky's best friend and brother-in-law, was buried next to his sister, Adrian, as seen in the film Creed. However, the gravestone for Paulie was Styrofoam and is no longer at the cemetery.

BOOK IT!

WHAT The Rosenbach

WHERE 2008–2010 Delancey Pl., Philadelphia 19103

COST Adults, $10; seniors (sixty-five and older), $8; students and children, $5; children under five, free

Do you read banned books?

Now considered the author's masterpiece, James Joyce's novel *Ulysses* was the center of controversy when it was serialized in *The Little Review*, an American periodical. One chapter, titled "Nausicaa," was considered obscene. The novel itself was banned in the United Kingdom and the United States until the 1930s.

So what does this have to do with Philadelphia? Well, Philadelphian A. S. W. Rosenbach had a first edition of *Ulysses* smuggled into the country in 1922. Today, a manuscript of the novel in Joyce's own hand is a favorite exhibit at the Rosenbach, home of one of the world's greatest collections of manuscripts, rare books, antiques, and works of art.

A. S. W. Rosenbach and his older brother, Philip, were renowned book and fine art dealers, and their own personal collections are the core of the Rosenbach. The museum is housed in two nineteenth-century townhomes, where the brothers resided until their deaths in the early fifties. Much of the house is furnished with eighteenth-century English

Come for the books; stay for the surroundings. The beauty inside the townhouses isn't just on the page. Soak in the wonders of the collections of fine arts, jewelry, and glass, showcased in a home full of antiques.

Open the door to a collection of rare books, fine art, and antique furnishings that will fuel the imagination. The Rosenbach seeks to inspire curiosity and creativity in everyone, from schoolchildren to scholars, young and old. Photo courtesy of the Rosenbach. Inset: Rare books, such as this copy of Poems, Chiefly in the Scottish Dialect, *by Robert Burns, are among the gems visitors discover during a visit to the Rosenbach. This volume was printed by John Wilson in 1786. Photo courtesy of the Rosenbach.*

furniture, as it was when the Rosenbachs lived there. One notable exception: On the third floor, you'll find poet Marianne Moore's Greenwich Village living room, which includes more than 2,500 of the Modernist's personal items.

Other items of note on display at the Rosenbach include Bram Stoker's notes and outlines for his novel *Dracula*, an extremely rare first edition of Cervantes's *Don Quixote*, and more than sixty letters written by President Abraham Lincoln, among many other rarities and wonders.

And a Ben Franklin sighting—the only known surviving copy of the 1733 first edition of *Poor Richard's Almanac* is a part of the Rosenbach collection.

74

THE HISTORY OF SCIENCE

Do you know what you don't know?

When I was a kid, I had a fascination with science. I remember my parents bought me one of those kiddie chemistry sets for Christmas one year, and I had a great time testing every liquid in the house with litmus paper to determine whether it was a base or an acid. My chemistry career ended abruptly when I tugged too hard pulling a plunger out of a test tube of hydrochloric acid and splashed my face. I was fine, but my parents shut the whole thing down.

But I never lost my fascination for the why behind things, which is why the museum at the Science History Institute is such a great find. Nestled among all of Philly's bigger, better-known museums, the institute offers visitors an understanding of the impact of chemistry and other sciences on society.

The Science History Institute (originally called the Center for the History of Chemistry, then the Chemical Heritage Foundation) was founded in 1982. It consists of the museum, a library, archives, a research center, and a conference center. It also has one of the largest fellowships for the history of science, hosting up to twenty fellows a year.

In the institute's Masao Horiba Gallery, you'll find ExhibitLab, an area for rotating focused displays. Exhibits such as Second Skin: The Science of Stretch and Domestic Plastics have appeared in ExhibitLab. Check the institute's website to see what is currently being featured.

The Science History Institute (formerly known as the Chemical Heritage Foundation) includes a library, museum, archive, research center, and conference center. Visitors are immersed in the history of science and technology through the institute's interactive exhibits. Photo courtesy of the Science History Institute.

THE HISTORY OF SCIENCE

WHAT Science History Institute

WHERE 315 Chestnut St., Philadelphia 19106

COST Free

PRO TIP Free guided tours are available the last Saturday of every month at 2 p.m. Museum hours are Tuesday through Saturday, 10 a.m. to 5 p.m., and the first Friday of the month (March through December), 10 a.m. to 8 p.m.

Exhibits at the institute answer questions both big and small—everything from "How does a crayon get its color?" to "How was the DNA code cracked?" Permanent exhibits include Transmutations: Alchemy in Art, featuring artistic representations of chemistry and alchemy in the seventeenth, eighteenth, and nineteenth centuries, and Making Modernity, which demonstrates the frequent and often surprising ways chemistry touches our everyday lives.

The institute also features a proud collection of rare books, artwork, and antique chemistry sets—all things that make chemistry less complex and more fascinating. A showstopper is the giant interactive periodic table, complete with videos, on a 3-D screen.

75

WHERE THE KOI ARE

WHERE THE KOI ARE

WHAT Shofuso Japanese House and Garden

WHERE Horticultural and Lansdowne drives, West Fairmount Park, Philadelphia 19131

COST Adults, $10; children, seniors, and students with college ID, $5; ACCESS cardholders and up to four guests, $2; children under three and active military with ID and up to five guests, free

PRO TIP Because it is an indoor-outdoor exhibit, Shofuso is open seasonally in warm weather. The season runs from April through October (although it may begin in late March; check its website for details). Open Wednesday through Friday.

Where's the most beautiful place to go barefoot in the park?

Sure, it's in West Philadelphia. But when I take off my shoes and enter the traditional Shofuso Japanese House, I feel transported to another country.

The history of the exhibit dates back to 1876, when a Japanese-style landscape was designed for the 1876 Centennial Exposition. Shofuso (its name means "Pine Breeze Villa") itself was built in Japan in 1953, exhibited at the MOMA in New York, and then moved to its current site. It opened here in Philly in October 1958 and underwent a major facelift in June 1976, in time for the bicentennial celebration.

A gift from Japan to our

The Japan America Society of Greater Philadelphia hosts a plethora of events at Shofuso, including bonsai workshops, Japanese tea ceremonies, pop-up beer gardens, and a variety of summer camps.

Shofuso Japanese House and Garden is a traditional Japanese house and garden, representing the history of Japanese culture in Philadelphia. The nationally ranked garden is peaceful and breathtaking, especially when the cherry blossoms bloom in the spring. ©Scott Lebeau

country to symbolize our friendship and the peace following World War II, the simple but beautiful building surrounded by lush gardens certainly invokes a peaceful feeling. And who needs to drive to DC? The landscape here is rich with cherry blossoms every spring, and the air is heavy with the delicious scent of magnolia.

The house itself is an interesting glimpse at another culture, but outside is where the real magic happens. Bamboo grows, bonsais are sculpted, and a school of koi swims to the surface.

Although a visit here won't take long, the time you spend at Shofuso Japanese House and Garden will be serene and peaceful. Upmost respect is shown for the house and grounds, even in the way you must remove your shoes before entering to preserve the wood and white mats. (Peds are provided if you aren't wearing socks.) And although the house is closed in autumn, it's worth a visit back to see the trees adorned in their best reds, yellows, and oranges.

76

RACING IN THE STREETS

Do you have the need ... the need for speed?

It's time to get in gear ...

"The Spirit of Competition" is the central theme at the Simeone Foundation Automotive Museum, an 80,000-square-foot showroom featuring more than sixty sports cars representing decades of racing. And these cars, a collection amassed over fifty years, are the top of the line. Only cars passing a stringent set of qualifications make it to the collection—each one has a history of road racing (no Formula cars here!). Every car has its original parts, and all are considered historically significant, associated with superior racing performance.

From the 1909 American Underslung Traveler to the 1975 Alfa Romeo Tipo 33 TT 12, the field here is deep and impressive. The exhibits are set up in thoughtful display collections. One grouping, Pre-World War I Racing, features speedsters such as the Stutz Bearcat and the Mercer Raceabout. Another features cars that won at Le Mans, the prestigious endurance race in which, until 1970, cars would be driven for a straight twenty-four hours, with the winner being the car that went farthest. And don't miss the Winner's Circle, showcasing a car from each of the five major

Twice a month, on the second and fourth Saturdays, the museum holds Demo Days. Cars are demonstrated outside (weather permitting), and guests can get up close and personal for pictures with select autos. Demo Days are included in the price of admission.

According to signage in the museum, the S series supercharged Mercedes-Benz cars were the most successful prewar sports racing cars of the marque. When Mercedes and Benz joined together in 1927, eight Sportwagen cars were produced—of which this is the lone survivor. Inset: Another car on display at the Simeone Foundation Automotive Museum is this 1964 Cobra Daytona Coupe. Only six of these iconic cars were built. Their streamlined design and power made them victors in major races. ©Scott Lebeau

RACING IN THE STREETS

WHAT Simeone Foundation Automotive Museum, one of the world's greatest collections of racing sports cars

WHERE 6825 Norwitch Dr., Philadelphia 19153

COST Adults, $12; seniors sixty-five-plus, $10; students with ID, $8

PRO TIP The museum is open Tuesday through Sunday. A three-acre lot provides plenty of parking.

competing countries—France, the United Kingdom, Germany, Italy, and the United States. Each of these cars was the best of the best in racing for its time.

Collectively, the exhibits represent the evolution of the race car and demonstrate how competition encourages improvement and innovation. Processes get streamlined, engines get better, cars get faster. Because of the competition, the car becomes the best it can be.

Are you along for the ride?

77

THREE COINS IN A FOUNTAIN

THREE COINS IN A FOUNTAIN

WHAT The Singing Fountain

WHERE Eleventh Street and East Passyunk Avenue, Philadelphia 19147

COST Free

PRO TIP The Singing Fountain is at the hub of a very vibrant neighborhood, great for shoppers and foodies alike. Street parking is available, though tight. Amish farmers markets are held there weekly, and numerous neighborhood events are held in the area year-round. Come by during the holidays, when the fountain is dressed as a Christmas tree.

Where can you find a peaceful oasis in the middle of the busy city?

In a city of some 1.57 million people, you may think it would be hard to find respite from the crowds. (And that's not even counting the tourists!) But you'd be wrong.

Despite the urban trappings, Philadelphia is also rich in green space—and not just the large areas like Fairmount Park. One perfect example of a hideaway right in the heart of a thriving neighborhood is the little triangular plot of land at East Passyunk and Eleventh streets, where you'll find (and maybe even hear) the Singing Fountain.

Now to that burning question—does the fountain really sing? The answer is a qualified yes. The Singing Fountain used to flow with music, everything from Sinatra to current pop. The area is a little quieter now, but there is still piped-in music coming from speakers nearby.

The Singing Fountain appears as an oasis in an active shopping and dining mecca. Visitors can relax and even enjoy a game of chess in the shadow of the fountain. Inset: The fountain is also the site of a Little Free Library (littlefreelibrary.org), a nonprofit book exchange designed to encourage a love of reading and community building. ©Mary Dixon Lebeau

The Singing Fountain is the centerpiece of the city's trendy East Passyunk neighborhood, a shopping and dining mecca that is home to some of the most authentic Italian restaurants around. The fountain itself has occupied this space for years, but it received a facelift in 2011 thanks to the Passyunk Avenue Revitalization Corporation, which breathed new life into the area by tearing down unsightly fencing, planting new trees, and adding up-to-date, welcoming seating.

The area around the Singing Fountain seems like the perfect place to sit down and rest after a busy day shopping in East Passyunk. There are even chess tables available for those who'd like to spend the afternoon challenging a friend. And if you feel like relaxing with a novel, a Little Free Library right near the fountain invites all visitors to take or leave a book.

CHILD'S PLAY

Where do the children go?

Much has been written about childhood inactivity, which contributes to childhood obesity. Kids in the twenty-first century don't go out and play like previous generations did. Instead, they live in a virtual reality, glued to screens.

Kids need to be kids—and that means playing. But in a big city like Philly, safety and space are major issues. Fortunately, there's a wonderland for outdoor play set aside for kids right in East Fairmount Park.

Smith Memorial Playground and Playhouse is committed to providing opportunities for unstructured free play for city kids. And when I say committed, I mean just that—the playground was opened on July 23, 1899, and has been furnishing the children of Philly a place to run, jump, yell, and have fun for more than a century. Funded through the wills of Richard and Sarah Smith (the same Smiths who paid for the Smith Memorial Arch), the playground provides six-and-a-half acres of land for kids' free play. Here you'll

---

The question here—"Where do the children go?"—is a reference to the Philadelphia band the Hooters, who had a hit song of the same name. They were the opening act at the Philadelphia part of the 1985 fundraiser concert Live Aid. And the answer is that the children go to Smith. In fact, 200,000 people (adults and children) enjoyed the playground in 2016.

For city kids, the Smith Memorial Playground provides a green oasis amidst the steel and concrete of the city. Here they can run, play games, and enjoy the outdoors in a safe environment. ©Scott Lebeau

CHILD'S PLAY

WHAT Smith Memorial Playground and Playhouse

WHERE 3500 Reservoir Dr., Philadelphia 19121

COST Free

PRO TIP Smith Memorial Playground and Playhouse is closed on Mondays.

find spinning jungle gyms, old-fashioned tire swings, gigantic teeter-totters, and tot lots for the under-five set. Little ones are also welcome to play in the four-story playhouse, where they'll find rooms full of toys, a big wooden train, and a kids' driving area.

But the major attraction at Smith is the great outdoors— and the giant wooden slide you'll find there. Added to the playground in 2005, the Ann Newman Giant Wooden Slide is thirty-nine feet long and thirteen feet wide. Kids slide down one, two, and three across, often holding hands as they go down.

79

A SHOT IN THE DARK

How did the Embargo Act of 1807 affect Philadelphia?

When President Thomas Jefferson signed the Embargo Act of 1807, banning the import of buckshot and other ammunition from Europe, a trio of Philly plumbers saw an opportunity. They decided to get in on the ground floor and built a shot tower to supply ammunition to area hunters.

Shot towers were home to a relatively new industrial process at the time. Before the use of shot towers, lead for shots was poured into wooden molds and then cooled. The British discovered that dropping molten lead from a high place caused the falling lead to form perfectly round balls. The plumbers—Thomas Sparks, John Bishop, and James Clement—utilized this concept when they built the Sparks Shot Tower, one of the first in the country.

The drop method revolutionized the making of musket balls, speeding up the production of ammunition. The

A SHOT IN THE DARK

WHAT Sparks Shot Tower, a historic shot tower

WHERE 111 Carpenter St., Philadelphia 19147

COST Free

PRO TIP This is a roadside attraction, easily seen by motorists on I-95. It is within walking distance of the Mummers Museum.

The tallest building in the city when it was built, the Sparks Shot Tower is 142 feet tall. The diameter is thirty feet at the base, tapering up to fifteen feet at the top. It opened on July 4, 1808, and is one of five remaining shot towers in the country.

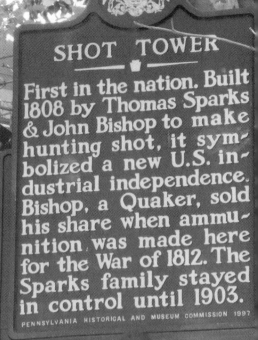

SHOT TOWER

First in the nation. Built 1808 by Thomas Sparks & John Bishop to make hunting shot, it symbolized a new U.S. industrial independence. Bishop, a Quaker, sold his share when ammunition was made here for the War of 1812. The Sparks family stayed in control until 1903.

PENNSYLVANIA HISTORICAL AND MUSEUM COMMISSION 1997

Though it hasn't been used to produce shot in more than a century, the Sparks Shot Tower has remained through the years and is now part of a city playground. Its base serves as a recreation center. When the brick tower was built more than two centuries ago, it represented a new technology in the production of ammunition. It is also South Philly's oldest standing industrial feature. Today, the entrance is sealed off to visitors. ©Scott Lebeau

federal government became a customer at the beginning of the War of 1812. This created a dilemma for partner John Bishop, who was a Quaker and couldn't support the war effort. Bishop sold his share of the business to Sparks; Clement eventually followed suit, and the Sparks family ran Sparks Shot Tower for four generations. They provided ammunition for both the War of 1812 and the Civil War.

In 1903 the business was sold to United Lead Company of Pennsylvania, and the company closed ten years later. The city of Philadelphia purchased the site in 1913, and it was added to the Philadelphia Register of Historic Places in 1956. It is now overseen by the city's Department of Parks and Recreation, sharing the corner of Carpenter and Front streets with a playground and recreation center.

80

OUR CITY, OUR TEAMS

OUR CITY, OUR TEAMS

WHAT Murals honoring Philadelphia sports teams

WHERE *Our City, Our Team* (the Eagles): outside Lincoln Financial Field on Darien Street; *76ers: Beyond the Court*: the intersection of Broad and Federal streets; *The Phillies Mural*: Twenty-Fourth and Walnut streets.

COST Free

PRO TIP If you're really into basketball, there's a mural honoring Doctor J. (Julius Erving) at 1234 Ridge Avenue in North Philly. Baseball fans can check out Jackie Robinson at 2803 N. Broad Street and Philadelphia Stars, a mural of the Philly athletes of the Negro League, at 4304 Parkside Avenue.

What's all the fuss about Philadelphia sports fans?

Ah, Philly sports fans. We've been known to be loud and crazy, forever hopeful, and a little crass. And yes, we were the ones who pelted Santa Claus with snowballs.

But all of that is because we're passionate. We love our teams—or love to hate them. Win or lose (and lose, and lose . . .), we stand behind them. If history is the soul of the city, then the Eagles, the Phillies, the Sixers, and the Flyers have to be the heart. (That's why so many of us bleed green.)

And that's why it's appropriate that some of our city's many murals immortalize our favorite teams. The latest is a 17,000-square-foot masterpiece across the street

The Phillies won the World Series in 1980 and 2008, and the 76ers took the NBA Championship title in '55, '67, and '83. Led by MVP QB Nick Foles, the Eagles won the Super Bowl in 2018.

The Phillies Mural, *painted by lifetime fan David McShane, features Hall-of-Famers, perfect games, and the Phillie Phanatic. The mural for the Eagles took some 386 gallons of paint and one thousand volunteers to create. The 76ers mural is a true community effort, with its design based on an entry from a local fifth-grader and a six-hundred-person paint day during the 2016 Democratic National Convention.* ©Mary Dixon Lebeau

from Lincoln Financial Field, home of the Philadelphia Eagles. In collaboration with the City of Philadelphia Mural Arts Program, the Eagles and their season ticketholders worked together with artists Phillip Adams and Jonathan Laidacker to bring their vision to life. The *Our City, Our Team* mural features an eagle soaring over the Ben Franklin Bridge, the team's training facility, and Lincoln Financial Field, and a variety of players and the city skyline. The fans are also given recognition, and you can practically feel their passion as you catch them in various poses of agony, ecstasy, and, always, hope.

Prefer baseball? *The Phillies Mural* towers over eight stories, facing the Schuylkill Expressway. Big moments in the team's history—including the 1980 and 2008 World Series Championships—are prominently featured. Basketball fans can find such notables as Allen Iverson, Wilt Chamberlain, and Charles Barkley doing their thing on the mural *76ers: Beyond the Court.*

<u>81</u> NYUK, NYUK, NYUK . . . WISE GUY, EH?

Can you name the Three Stooges . . . all six of them?

If you think museums are boring, you've never visited the Stoogeum.

The Stoogeum is the world's first and largest museum of Three Stooges memorabilia. Not just a personal collection on display, the Stoogeum is an expansive, interactive tribute to the Three Stooges brand and the comedy shorts of their era. And it's really fun!

The Stoogeum boasts nearly 100,000 pieces of Stooge memorabilia, from bobbleheads to puppets and shot glasses to schoolbags. There's also a theater where it's all Stooges, all the time, for those unfamiliar with the trio's short films (or those who just want to sit back and laugh at their slapstick vaudeville style).

Need to brush up on your Stoogeology 101? Start by poking fan favorite Curly in the eye and going through Stooge history on interactive computers. You can check out the filmology, appearances, and biographies of the Stooges and their cronies. You'll find the names of all six Stooges

NYUK, NYUK, NYUK . . . WISE GUY, EH?

WHAT The Stoogeum (it rhymes with "museum")

WHERE 904 Sheble Ln., Ambler 19002

COST Adults, $10; students with ID, $8; seniors sixty-five-plus, $8; children twelve and under, free

PRO TIP The museum is tucked away on a private street in a small office park. It's also only open on Thursdays, except by appointment. These things may make it easy to overlook, but don't! You may need to do a little digging to reach it, but like many rare gems, it's a great find. And there's plenty of free parking!

Left: Life-size statues of the best-known combination of Stooges—Moe Howard, Larry Fine, and Curly Howard—greet visitors to the second floor of the Stoogeum. Photo courtesy the Stoogeum.

Right: The world's first and largest museum dedicated to everything Stooges, the Stoogeum boasts a collection of thousands of pieces of Stooge memorabilia. Photo courtesy the Stoogeum.

here . . . the three Howard brothers, fuzzy-haired Larry Fine, Joe Besser (who joined the group following Shemp's sudden death), and Joe DeRita (known as Curly-Joe).

Displays include original costuming, personal effects, correspondence, and the Stooges' own scripts. The Hall of Shemp is dedicated to the often-maligned Shemp Howard, an original who had the unenviable task of filling in for an ailing Curly. (A plaque reads, "In Jewish culture, a boy becomes a man when he turns 13. In Stooge culture, it happens when he learns to love Shemp.")

And don't forget your quarters! Throughout the Stoogeum, you'll find Stooge-themed games, including a pinball machine, a video game, a gumball machine that promises a giant gumball if you feed a quarter under Larry's smiling face, and a Whack-A-Stooge, which is exactly what it sounds like!

The museum, which opened in 2004, is also headquarters of the Three Stooges Fan Club, one of the country's oldest fan clubs. The museum's curator, Gary Lassin, is married to Fine's great-grandniece, Robin.

Where can you find an eagle keeping a sharp eye on our money?

We all know that the bald eagle, a national symbol, has made appearances on our currency throughout the years. As early as the mid-1790s, eagles graced the reverse side of coins, and they are still "tails" on the Washington quarter. But did you know there once was an eagle overlooking our money even before it was made?

Legend has it that Peter the Bald Eagle lived at the Philadelphia Mint for six years—from 1830 through 1836. He became well known to the staff of our country's first mint, who gave him his name. Soon Peter had access to every room and vault in the building, and he often soared through the mint's rooftops in the evening following a day flying above Philly outside. Peter became a welcome mascot at the mint and was free to explore the vast building.

Unfortunately, the proud eagle fell victim to a freak industrial accident. A coining press on which Peter perched started suddenly, injuring the eagle's wing. Despite the best care available, the bird died of his injuries.

But Peter does live on—in memory, and at the mint. The beloved bird's stuffed remains are on display, and a bronze replica is perched nearby.

Peter isn't the only marvel you'll find when you tour the mint in Philly. Make sure to check out the historic artifacts at the country's first mint, including the first coining press, which was used to strike our new nation's first coins back in 1792.

UNITED STATES MINT

Self-guided tours of the United States Philadelphia Mint take approximately forty-five minutes to complete. During that time, visitors will view coining operations from forty feet above the production floor, see historic artifacts such as the coin press used to strike our country's first coins, and, of course, meet Peter. Unfortunately, no photography is permitted. ©Scott Lebeau

While visiting Peter's remains on your self-directed tour, be sure to check out the seven glass mosaics that detail the coining process of ancient Rome. The five-foot mosaics were created by Tiffany & Co. of New York in 1901 to celebrate the opening of the Third Mint Building.

Who's got a big appetite?

Anybody hungry? Yes, Philly has a lot to offer foodies—even beyond cheesesteaks and soft pretzels. But that's no secret.

What may come as a surprise is the giant food you can find in the city, not just in the restaurants, but on them, as part of the restaurant brand. One neat example is the giant olive that hangs on the side of the Continental Mid-town, a three-story Chestnut Street restaurant that specializes in the eclectic, the delicious . . . and the martini, of course. The giant green olive spiked with a toothpick hangs right outside the front door, an indicator of the retro vibe visitors will find within.

Tastykake has long been Philadelphia's preferred snack cake, but did you know you can find pie in the sky—a classic Tastykake apple pie, that is? Founded in 1914, Tastykake was once a local secret, available only in the Delaware Valley. The delicious Butterscotch Krimpets, Tasty Klairs, and Chocolate Juniors are available nationally now, but you can only find the giant apple pie outside the Tastykake Outlet Store on Venango Street.

Want ice cream? Then order your favorite frozen custard at the giant strawberry ice cream cone at Twistee Treat.

You can look down your nose at the giant olive from the gorgeous rooftop deck at the Continental. This restaurant is one of the many owned and operated by STARR Restaurants, the company owned by Stephen Starr, the 2017 James Beard Foundation Award winner for Outstanding Restaurateur.

Tastykake, founded in 1914, was an instant success. On its first day, the company sold twenty-two dollars' worth of snack cakes. At the end of the first week, sales were at $222, and by the end of the year, approximately $300,000 of the cakes were sold. ©Scott Lebeau

GIANT FOOD

WHAT Giant food . . . and the ants that follow

WHERE The Giant Olive: the Continental Mid-town, 1801 Chestnut St., Philadelphia 19103; Giant Tastykake Apple Pie: 2229 W. Venango St., Philadelphia 19140; Giant Ice Cream Cone: Twistee Treat, 3401 Longshore Ave., Philadelphia 19149; Giant Ants: 407 South St., Philadelphia 19147

COST Free

PRO TIP Twistee Treat is open seasonally, based on the weather. Check its Facebook page for operating hours.

The cone is a classic roadside attraction, one of ninety designed and fabricated in Florida in the eighties. This one arrived in Philly in the nineties, one of three that were brought here at the time. (There's another one still operating in Levittown, while the third no longer exists.) Place your order at one of the windows in the cone, then grab a picnic table to enjoy your treat.

And speaking of picnics . . . well, if there's giant food around Philly, can the giant ants be far behind? You'll find enormous sculpted insects crawling the building that used to house Zipperhead, the punk clothing and accessory shop made famous in a song by the Dead Milkmen. The store eventually relocated, but the ants still swarm, bugging the crowds on South Street.

Where can you find the best views of Philly?

The Philadelphia skyline is awe-inspiring. Just look out as the sun sets behind our magnificent cityscape, and keep in mind that this is the same city where our country was born, where freedom was proclaimed, where a bunch of rebels became "we, the people."

Yo, pretty amazing. Right?

Because Philly is such a sprawling city, there are many places to catch a great view. Not all are the same, of course, but each is beautiful and inspiring in its own way. Here are some of the best places to observe amazing views—and snap the best pictures—of the City of Brotherly Love.

• The Ben Franklin Bridge—If it's Philly, Ben Franklin has to be involved, right? But here's something you may not know about the Ben Franklin Bridge: It has a pedestrian walkway you can walk, run, or bike across. The path is above the cars on the bridge, so the view from the top is undisrupted. Sweet!

• The Philadelphia Museum of Art—After you do your best to run up the stairs Rocky-style, turn around and treat yourself to a gorgeous view of Center City and the Benjamin Franklin Parkway. (And while you're up there,

---

The Benjamin Franklin Bridge, which spans the Delaware River from Camden, New Jersey, to Philly, is a familiar sight to moviegoers. It has appeared in a variety of films, including Blow Out, Twelve Monkeys, Philadelphia, and, of course, Rocky.

Take a walk to the top of the Benjamin Franklin Bridge to get a great view of the Philadelphia skyscrapers over the Delaware River. ©Scott Lebeau

VIEW FROM THE TOP

WHAT Best views of Philadelphia

WHERE Various locations

COST Some are free, while others are fee-based as noted

PRO TIP The view from the top is always good, but the city is particularly beautiful when bathed in the gold and amber tones of sunset.

go inside. There's a whole lot more to the museum than those *Rocky* steps.)

• The 6ABC Zooballoon—Visitors to the Philadelphia Zoo have the opportunity to rise to heights of four hundred feet on the 6 Zooballoon. From that vantage point, you can get a bird's-eye view not only of the zoo but also of Center City and Fairmount Park. But take pictures quickly. The ride only lasts approximately ten minutes and costs twelve dollars a person.

• One Liberty Observation Deck—Want to see Philly from all sides? The best place to get a panoramic view is at One Liberty Observation Deck, where you'll see the city from all angles from the fifty-seventh floor. Tickets are fourteen dollars for adults and nine dollars for children ages three through nine.

85 CURTAIN TIME

CURTAIN TIME

WHAT Walnut Street Theatre, America's oldest theater, active since 1809

WHERE 825 Walnut St., Philadelphia 19107

COST $16 per person for the tour, held on scheduled spring and fall weekends. Prices for show tickets vary; check walnutstreettheatre.org for information.

PRO TIP Day-of-show tickets for Mainstage Productions, if available, are sold on the day of the performance for half-price online, by phone, or at the box office, using the promo code WSTDAY.

Where can you get a backstage pass for America's oldest theater?

Philadelphia's Walnut Street Theatre—the country's oldest theater—opened its doors on February 2, 1809, as an equestrian circus. The horses didn't hold center stage for long, though. By 1812 the building had been converted to a theater, thespians took over for the equestrians, and President Thomas Jefferson and the Marquis de Lafayette attended the opening-night performance of *The Rivals*.

Through the years, Walnut Street Theatre has been a trendsetter in live

Actor Edwin Booth, member of an illustrious nineteenth-century theater family, bought the Walnut Street Theatre in 1863. Two years later, his brother, actor John Wilkes Booth, assassinated President Abraham Lincoln at Ford's Theatre in Washington, DC. The Booth brothers' father, Junius Brutus Booth, made his own acting career at the Walnut Street Theatre.

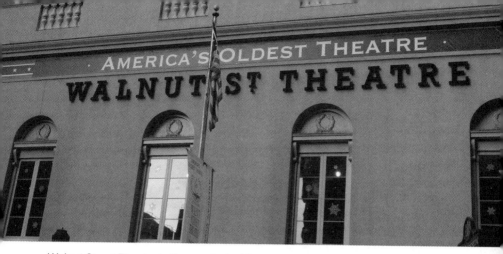

Walnut Street Theatre is the country's oldest continuously operating theater. It is a National Historic Landmark as well as the Official State Theater of Pennsylvania. ©Scott Lebeau

productions—it was the first theater in the United States to install gas footlights in 1837, the first to install air conditioning in 1855, and the site of the first curtain call, now a mainstay of theater productions worldwide.

The Shubert Organization purchased the theater in the 1940s, and it became the site of many pre-Broadway tryouts of plays that later became classics of the era. *A Raisin in the Sun*, starring Sidney Poitier; *Mister Roberts*, starring Henry Fonda; and Neil Simon's first Broadway effort, *Come Blow Your Horn*, all passed the audition at Walnut Street before heading to the Great White Way.

Declared a National Historic Landmark in 1964, Walnut Street Theatre was renovated in 1969 to become a performing arts center. Thousands of plays, musicals, dances, and concerts have been performed there. But this might be a secret: It was also the site of the first televised Carter-Ford presidential debate in 1976. Carter was awarded the Philadelphia Liberty Medal on the same stage in 1990.

Today, the theater boasts more than twenty productions each season. It's the world's largest subscribed regional theater company, and it has thriving educational and outreach programs. It continues to build on honored theater traditions while bringing the latest and greatest productions to the people of Philadelphia.

189

86

A (MOON) TREE GROWS IN PHILLY

Where can you find the mass graves of Revolutionary War soldiers?

Originally known as Southeast Square, the lush green park now known as Washington Square is one of the five drawn up by Philadelphia founder William Penn in his 1682 blueprint of the city. But early on, it became a burial field—and it remained such for more than ninety years.

Thousands of bodies of Revolutionary War soldiers, freed blacks and slaves, yellow fever victims, and "strangers" were buried in these grounds. First there were the strangers, visitors to the city who did not have ties to a burial ground or couldn't afford one. Next came the Revolutionary War soldiers, many of whom fought under General George Washington in battles nearby, then were brought, wounded or sick, to the city's hospitals. Thousands of soldiers were buried in mass graves, wooden casket upon wooden casket.

In 1793, the yellow fever epidemic devastated the area, and once again the square was used as a burial ground. After the outbreak had subsided, the square stopped being used

---

Another, more futuristic, attraction at Washington Square is the cloned Moon Tree. The original, a sycamore raised from one of the seeds carried to the moon by Apollo 14 astronaut Stu Roosa, was planted in 1975 but died in 2008. The current Moon Tree was cloned with the help of the staff at the Morris Arboretum, who rooted cuttings from the original.

An eternal flame burns at the Tomb of the Unknown Revolutionary Soldier, a centerpiece of Washington Square. The inscription on the tomb reminds visitors, "Freedom is a light for which many men have died in darkness." ©Scott Lebeau

as a cemetery. Beautification efforts began, and in 1825 the area was renamed Washington Square in honor of the general who had led so many of those buried there.

The Tomb of the Unknown Revolutionary Soldier was completed in 1957. It includes a monument featuring a statue of George Washington, an eternal flame, and the Tomb of the Unknown, which holds the remains of a soldier buried in the square. But here's an eternal secret . . . it's unknown whether the remains are those of a Colonial or a British soldier. The inscription on the tomb reads, "Beneath this stone rests a soldier of Washington's army who died to give you freedom."

A (MOON) TREE GROWS IN PHILLY

WHAT Tomb of the Unknown Revolutionary Soldier and Moon Tree in Washington Square Park

WHERE 209 W. Washington Square, Philadelphia 19107

COST Free

PRO TIP The Moon Tree is just yards away from the Tomb of the Unknown Revolutionary Soldier. NASA astronaut Stu Roosa assisted with the planting of the original Moon Tree in 1975, part of the bicentennial celebration.

87

TOOTHY GRINS

Who would wear a necklace made of teeth?

Here's a museum you can sink your teeth into! Part of Temple University, the Kornberg School of Dentistry devotes its third floor to the small, quirky Edwin and Trudy Weaver Historical Dental Museum.

Old-fashioned dental drills, X-ray machines, and other dental antiques—some ranging as far back as the late eighteenth century—will make visitors grateful for present-day technology. A re-created nineteenth-century Victorian dental office features an old-fashioned dental chair, period furniture, and instruments, while historic teaching methods include a plaque featuring blue wax teeth. Dental students needed to know the teeth intimately, and they had to create

TOOTHY GRINS

WHAT Weaver Historical Dental Museum of Temple University

WHERE 3223 N. Broad St., Philadelphia 19140

COST Free

PRO TIP The Dental Museum is closed weekends. Street parking is available.

Another exhibit traces the history of dentistry in America through three generations of one family—from Josiah Flagg, a Revolutionary War-era dentist, to his grandson J. Foster Flagg, who was a founder and member of the faculty of Philadelphia Dental College, which was the second-oldest dental school in the nation. It merged with Temple in 1907.

Talk about reusing! "Painless" Parker made this necklace of the molars, bicuspids, and other teeth he extracted. ©Scott Lebeau

a set of blue wax bicuspids, molars, and the like to graduate from dental school.

Perhaps the most absorbing tale is that of Edgar R. R. Parker, an 1892 graduate of Philadelphia Dental College (which is now the Kornberg School of Dentistry at Temple University). Parker, who legally changed his first name to "Painless," was frustrated at the lack of clientele at his own dental office, so he took his show on the road. "Parker Dental Circus" was part traveling roadshow, part mobile dental clinic, complete with sideshow entertainers and a dental chair on a horse-drawn wagon. After the crowd was entertained by a band and dancing girls, Parker would give a brief lecture on dental health care, followed by extractions (with the band playing loudly to cover up any signs of discomfort).

By the time he died in 1952, "Painless" Parker was perhaps the world's best-known dentist. At the museum, visitors can learn all about his story, as well as see a wooden bucket filled with teeth pulled by the showman/dentist. A necklace made of teeth (reportedly pulled by Parker on a single day) is also on display.

88

IT'S GOT A GOOD BEAT

What American music institution began in West Philadelphia?

Okay, "Will Smith" may be an acceptable answer to that question. But let's think back . . . way back . . . do you remember when rock was young?

Once upon a time, kids across the country tuned in every day to study the teens in Studio B at WFIL. They watched and they copied, mimicking the hairstyles, the Peter Pan blouses and bobby socks, and, most of all, the dance moves. Because, once upon a time, kids across the country wanted to be on *Bandstand*.

Now recognized as a rock and roll institution, *American Bandstand* started as the first record and dance party show on television. Back then, it wasn't even American—it was just Philly, and the show was known as just *Bandstand*. First emceed by a Philly disc jockey named Bob Horn, the show ran for four years before a young Dick Clark took over the hosting duties and turned the local after-school favorite into a national phenomenon. It was Clark who convinced ABC execs to give the show national exposure—and in 1957, *American Bandstand* was born.

For the following thirty-two years, the show ran continuously. Even though it moved to California in 1964, *Bandstand*'s early years in Philadelphia became the base for

The Dick Clark version of Bandstand aired locally for seven-and-a-half hours each week and was fed to the ABC network, making WFIL-TV the nation's largest single-station originator of network programming at the time.

AMERICAN BANDSTAND

his television program had a major impact on the music, dance, and lifestyles of merican teenagers. "Bandstand," a local ow, began in 1952. Dick Clark became ost in 1956, and on August 5, 1957, merican Bandstand" debuted on the tionwide ABC network. Until 1964 the ow was broadcast from WFIL-TV here. his 1947 building was one of the first esigned and constructed exclusively for levision productions.

PENNSYLVANIA HISTORICAL AND MUSEUM COMMISSION   2002

This building is the former home of WFIL Studio and Bandstand. *The network advertised itself as "WFIL-adelphia." ©Scott Lebeau. Inset: From the start,* Bandstand *was popular with its teenage audience in Philadelphia, capturing the culture, fashion, and dance trends of the city's young people.*

IT'S GOT A GOOD BEAT

WHAT Marker and building that once housed WFIL Studio, original home of *American Bandstand*

WHERE 4548 Market St., Philadelphia 19139

COST Free

PRO TIP The building is now the headquarters of the Enterprise Center, so there is seldom access for visitors. There is, however, a marker outside, and on rare special occasions, Studio B, where *Bandstand* was taped and memorabilia is stored, is open to the public. The most recent open house was in April 2012, following the death of Dick Clark.

its influence on the music industry, as well as a benchmark in the early days of television.

WFIL Studio was one of the first buildings in the world specifically designed for television broadcasting. The building still stands, although with new tenants, and is now on the National Register of Historic Places. A marker outside commemorates the impact the show and Dick Clark had on the music, dance, and lifestyles of the American teenager.

89

LIKE TALKING TO A WALL

How hard is it to keep a secret?

Ben Franklin once wrote, "Three can keep a secret, if two of them are dead." He may have added, "And if the remaining one never murmurs the secret to himself while standing near the Smith Memorial Arch."

Of course, old Ben didn't say that. He was long dead before the arch was first conceived in 1891. But he knew a secret is hard to keep—and that is proven big time at the Whispering Benches, which serve as the memorial's seating areas.

So, want to test it out? Bring a friend to the Smith Memorial Arch in Fairmount Park. Each of you take a seat on the stone benches, but at opposite ends, not next to each other. Then one of you whisper into the curved wall at your end. Your secret will be clearly heard by your friend at the opposite end!

The Smith Memorial Arch itself is a monument commemorating Civil War heroes from Pennsylvania. It was commissioned in the will of Richard Smith, who made a fortune as a type founder and donated half a million dollars for the construction of the arch.

The bronze and limestone memorial features fourteen separate figures created by twelve different artists. Highlighted prominently are such war heroes as General

LIKE TALKING TO A WALL

WHAT Whispering Benches at Smith Memorial Arch

WHERE Fairmount Park, in front of Memorial Hall (4231 Avenue of the Republic, Philadelphia 19131)

COST Free

PRO TIP The benches have become an iconic location for a couple to share their first kiss. Or, perhaps, whisper a proposal?

It works! If you whisper into the curved wall behind the Whispering Benches, the person on the other end of the bench will hear it perfectly. The way the stone is curved carries the sound from one end to another. Inset: Another secret of the Smith Memorial Arch: Richard Smith himself appears with the war heroes, even though he did not serve in the war. ©Mary Dixon Lebeau

George Gordon Meade, Major General George B. McClellan, and Admiral David Dixon Porter, among others. There are also two eagles perched on globes, a list of eighty-four Pennsylvania Civil War veterans, and, oddly, a figure of Richard Smith himself, who was not in the service during the war.

Apparently, Richard Smith and his wife, Sarah, liked to spread the wealth. Their estate also funded the Smith Memorial Playground and Playhouse, a Fairmount Park favorite.

Who rests under the nation's tallest tombstone?

Some people think that—in life and in death—"the bigger, the better." And that even comes down to tombstones. But the tallest tombstone in the country doesn't mark the grave of a beloved president, a renowned athlete, or a famous movie star. No, the country's largest actual tombstone (as opposed to a monument or memorial) is the fifteen-story-high obelisk marking the grave of Thomas Wiltberger Evans, a nineteenth-century dentist. And you can find it (pretty easily—it's tall!) in the Woodlands Cemetery, which sits on the west bank of the Schuylkill River in Philadelphia.

Even without the "biggest" distinction, the Woodlands is worth a visit. Originally part of the estate of Philadelphia lawyer Andrew Hamilton, the fifty-four acres of green fields now feature a unique eighteenth-century English pleasure garden and an expansive nineteenth-century rural cemetery. The Woodlands is a National Historic Landmark District and serves as a center for education and cultural

The living care for the dead here, as a group of 150 volunteers known as the Grave Gardeners cares for the plots during the gardening season. Each Grave Gardener adopts a cradle grave at the cemetery, planting Victorian-era plants at the site and caring for them for the season. Popular during the Victorian period, cradle graves were tombs with both a headstone and a footstone, connected by a blanket of living plants and flowers.

WHAT The Woodlands, home of the tallest tombstone in the country

WHERE 4000 Woodland Ave., Philadelphia 19104

COST Free

PRO TIP Having trouble finding Evans's plot? He is buried in Section M, Lot 6-15 of the cemetery. Just look for the obelisk, resembling a miniature Washington Monument.

Woodlands Cemetery Company of Philadelphia was founded in 1840. The fifteen-story obelisk on the gravesite of dentist Thomas Wiltberger Evans, who died in 1897, is the tallest tombstone in America. ©Scott Lebeau

enrichment for residents of and visitors to the University City and West Philadelphia neighborhoods.

The gorgeous cemetery grounds are a throwback to a more genteel era and a favorite of those embarking on Victorian outings. More than 30,000 people are buried at the Woodlands, still a working cemetery, including Civil War general John Joseph Abercrombie; Anthony Joseph Drexel, founder of Drexel University; artist Thomas Eakins; and abolitionist Mary Grew, among many others.

None, however, stand as tall in death as Evans, a prestigious Civil War-era dentist who pioneered the use of gold fillings. Upon his death in 1897, Evans left his estate to the University of Pennsylvania to start a school of dentistry. Of course, that was after funding the ninety-foot obelisk that marks his tomb.

INDEX